FOR THE RECORD IV

Even More ...
Encouraging Words for Ordinary Catholics

Also by Rev. J. Ronald Knott

An Encouraging Word: Renewed Hearts, Renewed Church
The Crossroads Publishing Co., 1995 (out of print)

One Heart at a Time: Renewing the Church in the New Millennium.
Sophronismos Press, 1999

Sunday Nights: Encouraging Words for Young Adults.
Sophronismos Press, 2000.

Diocesan Priests in the Archdiocese of Louisville. Archdiocese of
Louisville Vocation Office, 2001.

Religious Communities in the Archdiocese of Louisville. Archdiocese
of Louisville Vocation Office, 2002.

For the Record: Encouraging Words for Ordinary Catholics.
Sophronismos Press, 2003.

Intentional Presbyterates: Claiming Our Common Sense of
Purpose as Diocesan Priests. Sophronismos Press, 2003.

For the Record II: More Encouraging Words for Ordinary Catholics. Sophronismos Press, 2003.

From Seminarian to Diocesan Priest: Managing a Successful
Transition. Sophronismos Press, 2004.

For the Record III: Still More Encouraging Words for Ordinary
Catholics. Sophronismos Press, 2005.

Copies of Father Knott's books can be ordered via e-mail by sending a
request to scholarshop@saintmeinrad.edu or by calling 1-812-357-6571.

FOR THE RECORD IV

Even More ...
Encouraging Words for Ordinary Catholics

Rev. J. Ronald Knott

Sophronismos Press   Louisville, Kentucky

FOR THE RECORD IV
Even More ... Encouraging Words for Ordinary Catholics

First Printing: October 2006
ISBN #0-9668969-7-1

Printed in the United States of America

Morris Publishing
3212 East Highway 30
Kearney, NE 68847
1-800-650-7888

To Archbishop Thomas C. Kelly, OP, who has been my bishop and the epitome of encouragement in my ministry as a priest during his twenty-five years as leader of the Church of Louisville.

ACKNOWLEDGMENTS

I would like to thank Mr. Joseph Duerr, editor of The Record, our archdiocesan newspaper, for giving me the opportunity to write these weekly columns. I also thank Mr. Glenn Rutherford for editing these columns each week and for giving me valuable advice along the way. I would like to offer a special thanks to Ms. Lori Massey for further editing and also formatting these columns into a book. Last of all, I would like to thank the many supportive readers who have encouraged me to keep on writing and who have taken the time to let me know how much these words of encouragement have meant to them.

"I now feel a need to write to encourage you to fight for the faith that has, once for all, been handed down to the holy ones.

—Letter of Jude 1:3

Preface

It may bear fruit next year; if not, then you can cut it down. Luke 13:9

This is my 200th column, more or less, and concludes my fourth year of writing "An Encouraging Word" for The Record. Part of me wants to quit because it is so demanding to try to crank out 500 words every week with all the other work I have to do.

I spend a lot of holidays and late nights trying to keep up. I would also like to spare myself the angry attacks that a few hurl at me when they don't like what I write.

Another part of me feels the need to continue, especially when I seem to constantly run into people who tell me how much they look forward to reading the columns each week.

In this column, let me end my fourth year of column-writing by sharing a few bits of feedback from my fans. They are typical of the many, many responses I get.

"We look forward each week to your column, as does my mother-in-law. She was with us over Christmas and got attached to your writings. So each week, off goes your column to Wisconsin."

"I am 87 years of age and enjoy your column in The Record. Please send me all three of your books."

"I have a nephew, a Catholic school graduate, who has maintained for years that he does not believe in God and never has. I gave him a copy of one of your books. His mother now tells me that he has returned to the church, is active in his parish, and his young wife is in the process of converting. I have to believe that you planted the seed."

"I look forward to reading your words each week. I cut out interesting thoughts that you share with us and send them to my family and friends who do not have the opportunity to read your column."

"My friend and I are avid readers of your columns each week. She has been going through chemotherapy now for three years. Without knowing it, you have no doubt been there for her during some of her rough periods."

I even got a compliment from a priest. "Your column is great, a terrific addition to The Record. Frequently folks mention your column to me. They really read it. Your straightforward and honest approach resonates with people. I would assume that it is the paper's most popular feature. You have a formidable 'bully pulpit,' and you use it well."

The criticisms have been few, but sharp. Nobody can please all the people all the time. What I try to do is to read the criticisms carefully, look for ways to improve my communication skills and be open to learning from a different perspective.

The bottom line is that I have decided to continue for a fifth year. Besides, what would I do with all that time between 10 and midnight everyday, not to mention holiday afternoons?

September 29, 2006

Table of Contents

Many of Us have Wanted to Quit

I say to myself, I will not mention him, I will speak his name no more. But then it becomes like a fire burning in my heart, imprisoned in my bones; I grow weary holding it in; I cannot endure it. Jeremiah 20:9

I love stories about great saints who get so fed up with God that they finally "let him have it!" One of my favorites is about St. Theresa of Avila, maybe the greatest female mystic of our church.

She traveled around Spain trying to reform the convents of her order that badly needed renewal. It was her practice to go to the chapel before one of these long and arduous trips to pray for a safe trip. After one such trip, when everything that could go wrong did go wrong, she stormed into the chapel and yelled, "Listen, God, if this is the way you treat your friends, no wonder you have so few."

Another of my favorites is Jeremiah. As a young man, Jeremiah was called, against his will, to be a prophet. He tried to beg off, telling God he was too young, too inexperienced and totally unable to speak in public.

God would not accept his excuses. His prophetic preaching evoked deadly hostility. He was put in stocks, he was tried for blasphemy and he was imprisoned for desertion. He was even thrown into a well and left to die by his own relatives.

Jeremiah grew not merely tired of the abuse -- he steamed with frustration. "Listen, God, you sweet-talked me into this job and then you abandoned me. I am a laughing stock. Your message has brought me nothing but ridicule and rejection all day long. I don't even want to mention your name any more. I'm fed up. I'm finished. I'm out of here."

Then comes that famous "but" in his prayer. "I am furious with you on one hand, but then on the other hand your message is like a fire burning in my heart. It is imprisoned in my bones. I can't help myself. I couldn't quit if I wanted to."

Who hasn't wanted to quit – quit his church, quit his marriage, quit his job or quit being a parent?

It is easy to be ordained, fun to go through a first Mass, exciting to get your first parish. But one doesn't really decide to be a priest until he hits one of those darkest moments. It is then that one really chooses priesthood.

It is easy to be married when you are in love, when everything is exciting. But one really makes the decision to be married when the honeymoon is over, when you face a crisis in your marriage. It is then that you either commit or run.

As Jeremiah discovered, you don't answer a call once, but over and over and over again. You don't just say "I do" once, but "I do" again and again, especially in those dark and confusing times.

October 6, 2005

Forgive and You will be Forgiven

Peter asked Jesus, "Lord, how often must I forgive? As many as seven times?" Jesus answered Peter, "I say to you, not seven times but seventy times seven." Matthew 18

Like Charlie Brown himself, good old St. Peter craves affirmation. Like a needy little puppy looking for a pat on the head, St. Peter is always on the lookout for ways to impress Jesus. No matter how hard he tries, he seems to keep missing the mark over and over again. You have to love this big-hearted lug.

The stories of St. Peter embarrassing himself are numerous, but the one we have today is typical. Jesus had just told his disciples that they must forgive one another. When Jesus finishes speaking, imagining that another chance to impress Jesus has presented itself, good old St. Peter springs into action.

Peter knows well that the rabbis had always taught that people needed to forgive three times. Peter gets out his little adding machine and multiplies that by two and adds one for good measure. Then he asks his question and answers himself at the same time.

"How many times must we forgive? Seven times?" He obviously expected Jesus to say, "Wow, Peter, how generous you are! You are better than the best! Seven times is beyond the call of duty!" You can almost see his big eager grin melt when Jesus told him to forgive not seven times, but seventy times seven times. That is forgiving without counting the times.

The biggest mistake people make when it comes to forgiveness is thinking that forgiveness is for the benefit of the offending party. Forgiveness of others is actually a gift we give ourselves. Grudges

3

consume vast amounts of time and energy – the incessant mental energy of rehearsing it over and over in our minds, the constant retelling of it to anyone who will listen, the regular bad feelings it keeps generating.

While we are doing all this to ourselves, the offending person is probably unaware of the punishment we are inflicting on ourselves. As the comedian Buddy Hackett put it, "Don't carry a grudge. While you are carrying the grudge, the other guy's out dancing."

The second reason to forgive is also selfish – so that God will forgive us. The Book of Sirach lays it out quite clearly. "Forgive your neighbor's injustice; then when you pray, your own sins will be forgiven. Could anyone nourish anger against another and expect healing from the Lord?"

Jesus put it this way: "Forgive and you will be forgiven. The measure you measure with will be measured back to you." Holding a grudge is a dangerous, as well as self-defeating, thing to do.

How many old grudges are you carrying around in your mind and heart? Whom do you refuse to forgive? Isn't today a good time to cut yourself free, emotionally and spiritually? It may be the biggest step toward self-care you'll ever take.

October 13, 2005

Surround Yourself with the Wisdom of Others

Encourage one another. II Corinthians 13:11

The Beatles used to sing, "I get by with a little help from my friends." When I started writing this column more than three years ago, I did it to encourage ordinary Catholics during the dark early days of the sexual abuse scandal. Little did I realize that I was actually giving to others what I most needed for myself.

The words of Jesus have certainly come true for me – "Give and it will be given to you. Pressed down and shaken together will it be poured into your lap." The readers of this column have indeed been encouraging. They have poured it on. As Jim Stoval put it, "You need to be aware of what others are doing, applaud their efforts, acknowledge their successes and encourage them in their pursuits. When we help one another, everybody wins."

Besides the many good Catholics of this diocese, I have many friends who offer me encouragement as a writer-priest who lives alone most of the time. My house is sprinkled with yellow pads and journals, waiting for words of encouragement by way of a good quote. I have these affirming quotes stuck everywhere. As the poet Ovid put it, "The spirited horse, which will try to win the race of its own accord, will run faster if encouraged."

If you are not getting the encouragement you need, you might try this technique of surrounding yourself with the affirming quotes of others. If this technique is new to you, let me share a few samples from my journals. Some are insightful. Some are merely funny. All of them keep me going.

5

"Be a force of nature instead of a feverish, selfish little clod of ailments and grievances, complaining that the world will not devote itself to making you happy." (George Bernard Shaw)

"Be nice to your children (friends), for they will choose your rest home." "Housework can't kill you, but why take the chance?" (Phyllis Diller)

"It is useless to hold a person to anything he says while he's in love, drunk or running for office." (Shirley MacLaine)

"I can take reality in small doses, but as a way of life I find it much too confining." (Lili Tomlin as "Trudy")

"The best way to revive a church is to build a fire in the pulpit." (Dwight L. Moody)

"Some preaching is constipation of thought and diarrhea of the mouth." (Father Walter Burghardt)

"Those who think they can and those who think they can't are both right. Anyone who stops learning is old, whether this happens at twenty or at eighty." (Henry Ford)

"The bravest thing you can do when you are not brave is to profess courage and act accordingly." (Cora Harris)

"Impossible things just take a little longer." (Philo T. Farnsworth)

"Happiness is an inside job." (Dr. Bernie Siegel)

"Taking offense is just as destructive as giving offense." (Ken Keyes)

When you need encouragement and fail to get it from others, give it to yourself.

October 20, 2005

Making a Living or Learning How to Live?

We brought nothing into the world, nor have we the power to take anything out. I Timothy 6

Margaret, Ester and Mildred – rich widows retired in Florida – had created an informal support group after their husbands died. They were almost inseparable.

One day, out of the blue, Ester died of a massive heart attack. Margaret and Mildred stood by her casket at the funeral home, going over the good times they had together spending some of their vast amounts of money. In the conversation, Margaret leaned over and whispered to Mildred, "How much do you think she left?" Looking a little puzzled, Mildred whispered back, "All of it, Margaret! All of it!"

Indeed, "shrouds have no pockets."

Not too long ago, I saw a TV special about these rich Florida widows. It seems that many of their husbands died of heart attacks, pushing themselves unmercifully, trying to accumulate enough wealth so that they could "enjoy life" together in their old age. Making a living, so that they could enjoy life someday, had become so all-consuming that they had failed to savor life as they went along.

Nothing is as tragic as getting to the end of one's life and realizing that one has not really lived, but only struggled to get ready to live. The message of St. Paul to the young missionary, St. Timothy, is similar: There is a big difference between making a living and knowing how to live.

The Bible does not condemn making money, but teaches a balanced view of material possessions. What it condemns is the accumulation of wealth as a goal rather than as a means. Defending the usefulness of money, Margaret Thatcher, a former prime minister of

England, made this point, "Even the Good Samaritan would not have been much use to the man in the ditch unless he had some money in his pocket."

One of my favorite books, and one that teaches in detail what this reading teaches, is a book by Marsha Sinetar, entitled *Do What You Love and the Money Will Follow*. She teaches her readers not to focus on making money directly, but on being the best person they can be. She says her readers should follow that wise, whispering voice in their hearts that teaches what to treasure. If they do that, she says, the money will be there.

I learned an important lesson the second time I bought a new car. I was so excited about the happiness I thought it would bring. I found myself looking out the window at it the next day and saying to myself, "What was I thinking? I'm no happier than I was yesterday." It even depressed me a bit to look at it.

What really brings me happiness is my ability to relate to people in a loving way, helping them and being helped by them. I have found that when that has been my primary goal, I have always had more than I needed.

October 27, 2005

Our Weaknesses can be our Strengths

I will rather boast most gladly of my weakness, for when I am weak, then I am strong. II Corinthians 12: 9,10

"The priests' shortcomings simply cannot be concealed. On the contrary, even the most trivial soon gets known. For as long as the priest's life is well-regulated in every particular point, the intrigues cannot hurt him. But if he should overlook some small detail, as is likely for a human being on his journey across the devious ocean of life, all the rest of his good deeds are of no avail to enable him to escape the words of his accusers.

"That small offense casts a shadow over the rest of his life. Everyone wants to judge the priest; not as one clothed in flesh, not possessing a human nature, but as an angel, exempt from the frailty of others."

These words were not written by some self-pitying priest during the heat of the recent abuse scandal or by some priest who seeks to minimize the damage done to innocent victims. They were written by St. John Chryso-stom 1,500 years ago.

For my 25th ordination celebration, somebody enlarged an old photo of me right before I went into the Cathedral to be ordained. With eyes downcast, I look as if I was about to be hanged in the town square – either that or like one of those grooms in a cold sweat I have noticed as their brides come down the aisle.

I still remember what I was thinking in my last moments as a free man. I was thinking about how I was going to measure up to all the expectations people were about to place on me. I did not feel good enough then, and I do not feel good enough now.

No matter how hard I have tried, not feeling good enough has been a basic theme of my life. Father Nerinckx's words may be right on target, but they filled me with dread when he said, "Those who enforce the rules should be the first to keep them."

I have found my comfort, rather, in the words of St. Augustine when he said that "Christ's gift is not profaned by a weak minister, and what flows through him keeps its purity. What passes through him remains clear; what passes through defiled human beings is not itself defiled."

I am thankful that the validity of the message I preach does not depend on my personal goodness. That message is valid no matter how weak I am, and if I fail, blame me, not the path.

Sharing my weaknesses has been more helpful to those who have heard my preaching than any of the successes I have had on my own. Nobody wants to hear me whine about how bad I think I have had it. They do, however, want to hear about how to overcome similar problems in their own lives. As a priest, my weaknesses have been my strength.

November 3, 2005

Do We Realize how much God Loves Us?

He gave everybody a full day's pay. Matthew 20

Of all the parables of Jesus, this is one of my very favorites. A parable is a little, made-up story to make a point about God. Jesus came to reveal God, and because his audience was made up of simple people, he made up little, pointed stories as a way to get his message across. It was a way to help them understand something they didn't know by comparing it to something they did know.

The point that Jesus makes about God here is that God is nuts about us. The hero in this little parable is a vineyard owner. Jesus' listeners were familiar with vineyard owners, but the owner in this story seems a little crazy. You know what this owner did? He gave all his workers, even those who came in at quitting time, a full-day's pay no matter how much or how little they worked for him.

There were two different audiences listening to Jesus, and he wanted both to hear him. He spoke to the "religious types," the ones who kept all the rules, and to the "non-religious types" who couldn't, wouldn't or hadn't kept the rules.

This message outraged the "religious types" who thought that God should love them more because of all they had done for God. To them it was bad news. It was unfair. The "non-religious types" were bowled over to hear that God loved them with all his heart, in spite of the fact that they had done so little for God. To them it was good news. It was not about fairness, but generosity.

If Jesus wanted us to know that God loves us no matter how much or little we do for him, that a pretty mind-blowing message. It sounds unbelievable, too good to be true. Because it sounds too good to be true, many cannot accept it. They say he must not have meant what he said. So, we try to help it make sense by adding a list of "yes, buts," playing down the radicalness of this mind-blowing good news, saying, "Yes, God loves you unconditionally — but, if, when, except."

The reason so many religious types are threatened by this parable is their fear that if people start believing that, they will do anything they please. They believe that what people really need is the fear of God. Fear is what will keep them in line, these people say. But what really happens is when people finally "get" this incredible message is really the opposite. People want to change their lives. They will "hunger and thirst" for holiness in the broadest sense of the word.

How about you? Do you believe the message of this parable? Do you "get it" – that God already loves you? Once you accept that, once you begin to live out of that knowledge, God will slowly turn your life around. You will begin, maybe for the first time in your life, to love God, your neighbor and yourself with all your heart.

November 10, 2005

A Way to Build a Less Violent World

With all humility and gentleness, strive to preserve the unity of the spirit through the bond
of peace. Ephesians 4:2,3

I am just as impressed with King Abdulah of Jordan as I was with
his father, King Hussein. King Abdulah recently gave a speech at
The Catholic University of America in Washington, D.C. He said
some fresh and wonderful things in that speech:

"Muslim political and religious leaders must fight to take back our
religion from vocal, violent and ignorant extremists who have tried to
hijack Islam over the last 100 years. They do not speak for Islam any
more than a Christian terrorist speaks for Christianity. At one time
or another, all religions have faced extremists who abuse the power of
faith."

Wouldn't it be wonderful if the leaders of the world's religions would
stand together against extremism within their ranks and set an example
for their followers in honest, open and respectful dialogue? What if
we not only agreed to disagree, but also agreed to offer each other
respect and reverence in spite of our disagreements? From there, we
could build a less violent world.

The infighting in the Catholic church today is just a milder version
of that same extremism that has at its base a twisted and misplaced
defense of a narrow understanding of religious purity.

If priests are not part of the solution, they are part of the problem.
Pope John Paul II said that priests must be "men of communion." Sadly,
some priests, in their zeal for a narrow and personal definition of orthodoxy, are actually adding to our division and disunity, picking and

choosing from church teaching ideas that support their understanding of truth and conveniently overlooking the teachings that don't. Sad as well are the priests at the other end of the spectrum who are doing the same.

Vatican Council II said that priests have been placed in the midst of the laity so that they will lead them all to the unity of charity. It is their task to bring about agreement among divergent outlooks. They are guardians of the common good and promoters of unity.

The Congregation for the Clergy said in 1999 that a priest must never be a part of an ideology or of a faction. He must always move from a personal point of view to a communal point of view.

Pope Benedict XVI may have offered us the solution when he spoke recently to Orthodox and Protestant leaders – "unity in multiplicity and multiplicity in unity."

Cardinal Avery Dulles put it this way: "The conflict between the liberal and conservative wings has markedly politicized the church. Both sides are tempted to subordinate an even-handed concern for truth to the demands of a party spirit in which every action and statement is evaluated according to whether it supports one cause or the other. In spite of the agitation from both extremes, the Catholic church remains a communion of tradition and authority, open to dialogue and progress."

November 17, 2005

Gratitude is an Emotion that Can be Taught

Serve the Lord, your God, with joy and
gratitude for abundance of every kind.
Deuteronomy 28:47

Thanksgiving is not just a holiday, but an attitude that we should cultivate all year 'round.

Believers not only have that attitude, but we also know whom to thank. When we attend the Eucharist every week we should know that every Sunday is "thanksgiving day." The word "eucharist" means to "give thanks."

An attitude of gratitude does not seem to come naturally. It has to be taught. There is a story about a mother who spent the whole day with her six-year-old son at his favorite museum. On the way home, they stopped for hot chocolate, then checked out a new toy store that was giving away helium balloons. As they were leaving, the little boy asked his mom to buy an action figure for him. When she said no, he threw a fit.

After a whole day that had been devoted to his pleasure, there was no thanks, no appreciation, just "I want more, right now!" This woman has a familiar complaint. "We give our kids so much, and the more we give the less they seem to notice. They take it for granted."

When a child learns to be genuinely appreciative, she has reached the point when she realizes that she is not the center of the universe. Though babies are focused on their own needs, by age two children should be able to understand that giving – as well as getting – is part of a healthy life. Gratitude is a teachable skill.

Sadly, many of us never grow out of our childish ingratitude. When we are so used to getting what we want and wanting even more, we often forget to stop and remember the blessings we have, where they came from or the sacrifice others have made. Childish adults come to believe that the world owes them a living. This self-centeredness makes gratitude impossible.

Sadly enough, too, is that favorite American mantra: "I earned it, and since I worked so hard to have it, I have no one to thank but myself." When we do that, we have forgotten one important fact: If it were not for the generosity and sacrifice of others, not to mention the providence of God, we would never have been in a position to earn or work for anything.

Some people seem to believe that gratitude is an attitude reserved to those times when everything is going well. We can be grateful, even in want and difficulty.

Job is a perfect model for this kind of gratitude. When he had the world by the tail, he was grateful. When he lost almost everything, he was grateful. When his own wife suggested that he "curse God and die," he responded, "We accept good things from God, why should we not accept evil?"

It is good to have a national day of thanksgiving, but our gratitude should never be limited to one such day.

November 24, 2005

Being Rude to Each Other is a Growing Trend

Blessed are the merciful. Matthew 5:7

Meanness is rampant. From so-called frivolous lawsuits to rude and crude public behavior, civility and good manners are vanishing. The Courier-Journal printed an article recently saying that, according to a recent poll, 70 percent of the population agrees that people are more rude today than they were 20 or 30 years ago, and it is getting worse. This trend is noticed in rural as well as urban areas.

There is a tendency in public discourse these days as well to be in-your-face and angry. With little room for an honest and open discussion, political elections are a disgrace with their ever-widening bitterness and hostility. There is a tendency in public discourse to scold. No teacher, bishop, pastor, principal, parent or public figure is spared being publicly ripped apart, personally and professionally.

This trend is infecting the church as well. There is a style of preaching coming back that is characterized more by scolding than by encouragement. Preachers who employ this technique tend to believe that they can get people to reform by angry condemnations, by beating them over the head with the law and by threatening them with punishment. Their techniques, I believe, are self-defeating.

Jesus did not go there. He sought out the lost sheep, carried him home on his shoulders and asked people to rejoice with him for rescuing the lost sheep. He did not serve up lamb chops for dinner.

He ran down the road to meet the prodigal son, wrapped him in robes and gave him a ring for his finger. He threw a welcome home party. He did not ground him for two years. He did not believe in breaking the bruised reed or quenching a sputtering wick. In hopes of turning them around, he welcomed sinners and ate with them.

17

I suppose a few would rather read a column about all the things wrong with the church and the people in it – one that would lay down the law and point the finger at the law breakers. In this column, I choose to see the glass as half-full, not half-empty.

I choose to stand in awe of the good that God has wrought in our world. I choose to celebrate and give thanks for what is good about our people, our mission and our church. From the feedback, it seems to be working. People are reporting personal progress in discipleship from reading this "encouraging word."

Each year, including this year, I have published collections of these columns in books for people to re-read and share with others. "For the Record III" is just back from the press. A few copies of the previous For the Record" publications are still available. They are available for pick-up for $10 each at The Record office at the Maloney Center, 1200 South Shelby Street in Louisville. They also are available online (plus postage and handling) through scholarshop @saintmeinrad.edu. Profits will go to support seminarians.

December 1, 2005

Don't Cull the Herd; Build a Bigger Pasture

Go out into the main roads and invite to the feast whomever you find, good and bad alike. Matthew 22:9,10

There are some in the church who believe that we went "too far" in carrying out the mandates of Vatican Council II. The chaos that inevitably follows dramatic change is scaring them. Instead of understanding it as part of the breakdown that precedes a breakthrough, they see it as a collapse that can only be stopped by going back.

I look at it differently. I've been through enough moves to know how disruptive change can be. I have experienced change as a four-stage thing.

The first stage is the excitement of the dream. The second stage is disillusionment and regret for having set out. The third stage is the decision stage where you either choose to keep going or turn back. Depending on that choice, the fourth stage is moving into your dream or living in the past. This is true for moving, renovating a house, retiring or for a major shift in our understanding of church.

One of the things that aggravates me about people who want to go back is their willingness to drive the marginal and alienated out of the church instead of going after them. I have heard from more than one source a line of thinking that says it is worth reducing the size of the church for the sake of purity.

In light of today's parable, as well as the parables of the lost sheep, prodigal son and vineyard workers, that kind of thinking makes me cringe. Instead of culling the heard, why don't we build a bigger pasture?

"Dear Abby" had some good advice several years back. "Abby" said that the church is more of a hospital for sinners than it is a communion of saints. I could not agree more. Jesus did not beat people over the head with their sins, but forgave them and invited them to move closer to God. "Those parts of the body that we consider less honorable we surround with greater honor." (St. Paul)

People are not motivated to change by harsh condemnation. Such condemnation usually solidifies them in their bad choices.

I believe that we are the servants who are sent out with hands full of invitations for the good and bad alike. We are not the ones doing the inviting, but only the ones called on to deliver the invitation. It's not our party.

Let me end today's column with a little poem someone sent me a long time ago. It summarizes what I have been trying to say. It's called "Surprise."

I dreamed Death came the other night and Heaven's gate swung wide.
With kindly grace an angel ushered me inside.
And there to my astonishment stood folks I'd known on earth,
Some I'd judged and labeled "unfit," of little worth.
Indignant words rose to my lips, but were never set free,
For every face showed stunned surprise; no one expected ME.

December 8, 2005

20

Jesus brings the Triumph of Peace over Worry

Have no anxiety at all. Let the peace that God gives guard your hearts and minds. Philippians 4

He's got to be kidding! No anxiety at all?

With an expensive and iffy war raging in Iraq, with a mushrooming national debt, with thousands of poor people displaced in the South by one hurricane after another, with a sexual abuse scandal that won't quit, with cancer, AIDS and new strains of deadly flu on the way, with one political scandal after another, how can we possibly live St. Paul's words in today's church and world? How can we possibly remain anxiety free in the middle of all these storms?

"Anxiety" is a state of intense, often disabling apprehension, uncertainty and fear caused by the anticipation of something threatening. It not about what is happening or what has happened; it's about what might happen.

My dear mother comes to mind when I think of anxiety. It seems that she always had a thin stream of fear trickling through her mind. I can still see her in my mind's eye picking at her lower lip, a nervous habit that always accompanied moments of intense anxiety. I can still remember one time when we laughed at her for being so anxious. She snapped back, "Well, somebody around here needs to worry."

When I was about to be ordained, anxiety was very much on my mind. The church was undergoing a great upheaval, and priests were beginning to leave in significant numbers. I asked myself many times in that year leading up to ordination, "How am I going to keep my cool in a fast-changing church and in a world coming unglued? How will I be able to stay focused when one problem after another is going to be hurled into my face from both inside and outside the church? How will I be able to calm others when I seem to be torn up all the time myself?"

I have spent my life as a priest searching for an innermost calm that no storm can shake. When I discovered and admitted to myself that I cannot control what happens in the world, I knew I had to find a way to control my reaction to what happens out there. As one spiritual teacher said, "It is easier to put on slippers than it is to carpet the world."

A close relationship with Jesus brings that peace. If you truly believe that you are loved without condition, that God is on your side and holds no grudges, that in the end things are going to turn out OK because God has told us so, then a great peace will come over you. No matter how bad things get sometimes, no matter how much you have to handle, no matter how great your losses, you will know in your heart of hearts that you are in good hands because you are in God's hands.

As trust in God grows, anxiety fades proportionally.

December 15, 2005

Women Play an Important Role in the Church

The woman who fears the Lord is to be praised. Her value is beyond pearls. Give her a reward for her labors and praise her at the city gates. Proverbs 31

Women have played a very important part of my life, both growing up and as a priest. Every time the Scriptures give me an opportunity, I like to show my appreciation by celebrating their value in my own life and in the life of the church.

My mother was a model of selflessness. She would give the shirt off her back, not only to us kids, but to our relatives, neighbors and friends as well. She taught me how to say my prayers. I can still remember standing near a wood-burning stove in our old house as she rehearsed the "Hail Mary" with me for my First Communion.

I had a special relationship with my grandmother. She was a country midwife and baptized me when I was born and was in danger of death. She "had time for me" and taught me many practical things.

The Sisters of Charity of Nazareth played a huge role in my growing up. Not only did they teach me how to read and write and add and subtract, they taught me how to love God and live in his presence. I used to "hang out" with them sometimes, even when school was out. They always made me feel that I was valued and valuable. I loved them then, and I love them now.

The woman in today's reading is held up as "worthy, industrious, resourceful, generous, deserving of praise and reward." She is a model of resourcefulness in the midst of scarcity, something I have especially admired in the country women of my childhood. Dolly Parton sings in "Coat of Many Colors" about her own mother who made her a prized coat from donated rags sewn together. Women, especially, have always had to be resourceful.

In the explosion of lay ministry, it has been women who have taken on the lion's share of the work that used to be done by nuns and even priests. Of the 30,000-plus lay ministers currently working in parishes, some 80 percent are women, and their numbers are booming. Many women are now even leading priest-less parishes. As Margaret Thatcher once said, "If you want anything said, ask a man; if you want something done, ask a woman."

Melanie Sullivan, with whom I work at Bellarmine University, is one of those women. She is doing a great job of leading our campus ministry program, a program that was always led by a priest before her.

I have no idea where the church will be when the dust settles on the upheaval we are experiencing these days. I do know three things: we all need to remain faithful, we need everyone's gifts and God is in charge of where we are going.

I am proud to say that I have always had great female friends in my life.

December 22, 2005

The New Year and a New Beginning

See, I make all things new. Revelations 21:5

I always do my "spring cleaning" over the Christmas holidays. I clean off the desk, clean out the computer files, throw a lot of paper away, get rid of clothes that don't fit anymore and give away all that extra candy and other sweets that have accumulated over the holidays. I like to start the New Year freshly organized. I like that sense of a new beginning.

I usually end this cleaning frenzy with a personal New Year's Eve retreat. Instead of partying like the extrovert I'm not, I like to stay home alone like the introvert I am. I like spending New Year's Eve with God, thanking him for last year and asking for his direction for another year.

One thing I like about New Year's Eve is the sense that I can start all over again, from scratch. With God, no matter how bad last year was, no matter how many sins I committed yesterday, today I can start all over again. With God, there is always forgiveness and hope.

I know from 35 years of priesthood that many will go into the New Year with feelings of hopelessness. In fact, suicide is highest at this time of year. In this column, I want to speak directly to those of you who are tempted to give up, who are overwhelmed with feelings of hopelessness. My words to you are simple: don't give up, no matter what.

When I think back over my life, I remember many times when I wanted to give up. With God's grace, somehow I didn't give in to those feelings.

When I went off to the seminary at age 13, almost no one believed that I would make it, not even my pastor. What if I had given up then? When I had been in the seminary for only a year, the head priest threatened to send me home, calling me "a hopeless case." What if I had accepted his evaluation and quit?

When I was sent to the "home missions" for my first assignment, I wanted to quit. What if I had? What if I had given in to those feelings?

When the Cathedral cracked and almost fell to the ground, I felt like quitting. What if I had? When the sexual abuse scandal hit, I wanted to quit again. What if I had given into those feelings?

During those times, I remembered an old story about an engineer who designed a famous tunnel. He came up with the risky idea of digging from both ends and meeting in the middle. When the day came when the diggers were supposed to meet, they didn't. Thinking he had made a terrible mistake, he killed himself. On the day of his funeral, the diggers did meet, and the tunnel was perfect. The poor engineer had given up one day too early.

Don't give up no matter what. This could very possibly be your best year ever.

January 12, 2006

Making Good Use of the Time We Have

Rejoice always. Pray without ceasing. Give thanks in all circumstances. Do not quench the Spirit. Do not despise prophecies. Test everything. Retain what is good. Refrain from all evil. 1 Thessalonians 5

How much time do you have left? You don't know, do you? You may have 40 years or more, or you may have 40 hours or less.

Since I have no control over how long I will be here, I decided years ago that the only control I have is to live well each and every day. I decided that this is where I will put my energy, living well as I go along, not trying to predict when the end will come. I want to "be ready," not "get ready."

St. Paul has some good advice on "how to live while you wait." His advice is very helpful even today. He said:

- "Rejoice always." That does not mean that we should all be going around grinning like Cheshire cats, denying the painful realities of the world. It simply means that underneath it all, underneath all the pain, suffering, disappointments and set-backs, there is the certain knowledge that in the end, everything will turn out OK because God said so.

- "Pray without ceasing." This does not mean that we need to become religious fanatics. It means simply to live in a permanent state of awareness of God's love and presence as we go about our lives.

- "Give thanks in all circumstances." It is possible to be thankful, even in times of tragedy. One of the most stunning things we saw in New Orleans and similar places last year was the number of people who were interviewed in the most dire circumstances who reported that they were "thankful."

- "Do not quench the Spirit." God constantly invites us to be open to new directions, new happenings and new people. As I look back over my life, I am amazed at the great things that God sent to me when I opened my mind and heart to something I had never thought of!

- "Do not despise prophetic utterances." Prophets are people who tell us the truth whether we like it or not. To live well, we have to be open to hear things about ourselves that we would rather not hear. In truth, people who tell us what we want to hear are not necessarily our friends, and those who tell us what we don't want to hear are not necessarily our enemies.

- "Test everything, keeping what is good and rejecting what is bad." Like the Thessalonians, everything both good and bad is laid at our feet. We have to be discerning about what to keep and what to reject. We have to pick out what is truly good from those things that merely look good.

None of us knows how long we will be here on this earth, but we do have a choice about how we will live while we are here.

January 19, 2006

A Good Homily has a "Golden Nugget" Inside

They were spellbound by his teaching. Luke 4:32

The primary task of the priest, according to Vatican Council II, is to preach the Gospel. Since then, the preaching that takes place within the Mass has become known as a "homily."

Like much of Vatican II that was not new but a return to something much older, we have Origen (185-253) to thank for the word "homily." A *homilia* was a popular exposition and application of the scriptures read or sung in the liturgical assembly. The homilia remained popular from the third to 12th centuries.

From the 12th century until the 20th century, the pulpit became a platform for theological debate, denunciation of heresies, catechetical lectures and moralistic tales from the lives of the saints. The ancient tradition of preaching from Scriptures was not revived by the Council of Trent. The preaching that prevailed after the Council of Trent was often based on outlines of doctrinal topics with little or no reference to the biblical texts of the liturgy.

The revival of the *homilia* at Vatican II is, of course, closely connected to the influence of "the biblical movement," which restored the use of Scripture in general.

After 35 years of writing and keeping homilies, I still have almost all of them on paper. Stacked together, all that paper is taller than I am. As you might suspect, anyone who has produced as many homilies as I have has developed a certain style or method. I thought it might be interesting to give an inside view of how one priest goes about producing a "homily." Simply put, I always start in the middle, then I go to the opening and finally to the ending.

A homily is always based in the Scripture readings of the day, so the first thing you have to do is to read the Scriptures many times over. I call it "going over the texts with a metal detector." This process typically "sets off an alarm." Once identified, it is this "golden nugget" that one mines. It is this spiritual insight that becomes the body of the homily.

Once the body of the homily has been established, I like to look for an experience from everyday life that is connected to or helps introduce the idea mined from Scripture. The opening prepares people to hear something they do not know by comparing it with something they do know. In any regard, the opening must enlighten what the body is going to say, not be just any funny joke or story to "loosen up the crowd."

Finally, the homily ends with an application to the lives of ordinary people. Since a *homilia* is a "popular exposition and application of Scripture," not a theology lecture, this is where the whole effort fails or succeeds. No matter how smart he is, if a homilist is not in touch enough with non-elite peoples to communicate his knowledge to them, then that person should probably try a different ministry.

January 26, 2006

Compliments are a Good Thing to Pass Along

God gives to all generously and ungrudgingly.
James 1:5

Are you stingy with compliments and don't know why? Have you ever caught yourself purposefully withholding a compliment, even when you knew it could provide someone with a badly needed lift?

Maybe a friend has lost weight and really looks good. You notice it, and you know they would love for you to tell them that you notice it, but you catch yourself deliberately withholding verbal acknowledgment because you feel good about your own weight.

You and your roommates decide to throw a party, but only one of you actually does anything to make it happen. That one friend purchases the food, cooks and decorates. When the time for the party comes, you and your friends are shocked and amazed, but no one says anything to the one who did all the work because they feel that giving a compliment would expose their own laziness.

Your best friend gets a promotion at work, maybe the third since you have received a promotion. You know she is proud and would love to hear a compliment from you, but you withhold it because every time she gets a promotion, you feel smaller and smaller about yourself.

Even priests are notorious for their inability to compliment each other — something that goes all the way back to the apostles. When James and John made a move for the best positions in the kingdom-to-come, it says the others were "indignant" that they would dare try to get one step ahead of the rest.

Father Andrew Greeley, a highly successful writer and speaker, says in one of his books that the "worst thing a priest can do in front of his fellow priests is to be really good at something." He says "priests are reluctant to applaud the work of other priests for fear it will take away something from themselves."

If we really pay attention to our reactions to others, we would all probably have to admit that withholding compliments is something we do regularly. These compliments can be withheld even from our own brothers and sisters, spouses, parents, kids or best friends.

Why do we withhold compliments from each other? Compliments don't cost anything — or do they?

There seem to be two primary motivations for withholding compliments.

The main reason for withholding comes from a perception that if I praise you, I will not appear to be as good as you.

The second reason for withholding is that while I know you deserve to be complimented, I withhold it as a passive-aggressive way to punish you for some past behavior. You may have slighted me sometime in the past or you may be getting, in my estimation, too many compliments already.

If we pay close attention to our reactions to others, we can not only see our patterns of withholding, but we can also choose to rise above our selfishness and give others the badly needed lift they deserve and need.

February 2, 2006

Most TV Celebrates
the Worst about Us

I have set before you life and death, the blessing
and the curse. Choose life, then, that you and
your descendants may live. Deuteronomy 31:19

I have always been suspicious of flu shots given at malls and grocery stores, but even more so this year. I got my flu shot early, but
spent two weeks over Christmas laid up with the flu. I want my $30
back!

When I have the flu for that long, there's not much to do but sleep
and watch TV. I find it almost impossible to concentrate on things
such as reading or writing. I slept as much as I could, and then I sat in
front of "the box" and filled my head with mindless stupidity until I
couldn't stand another minute of it.

I hadn't watched that much TV since the last time I had the flu, and
I had forgotten just how awful it can be. It's not even junk TV; it's
garbage TV.

I learned that for merely $19.95 I could purchase 70 hours of
"blood-sucking, flesh-eating, bone chilling, horror classics" on just one
"collector's edition" DVD, if I acted "now."

I watched an Australian idiot poke at alligators until they snapped,
almost taking off his head. I listened to an incredibly arrogant political
talk-show host who promised "no spin." After a few minutes, my head
was spinning so badly that I had to run to the bathroom for relief.

There was one back-stabbing, cut-throat, humiliating "reality" show
after another. There were grown men with juvenile sexual obsessions
that would have embarrassed most teenage boys. There were the
celebrity-worshipping and scandal-hunting so-called "news" programs.

Jerry Springer's "guests" are an endless stream of pathetic examples of humanity who have no idea which of a hundred relatives and casual acquaintances is "my baby's real father."

You can tour the incredibly gaudy and tasteless mansions of some obscenely overpaid music stars. I haven't been that nauseous since I toured the Elvis mansion, in disguise, back in the '70s.

You can watch young adults eat cockroaches and wallow with rats for prizes on "Fear Factor." You can watch parents sue their own children for $150 on "Judge Judy" and see people lie about lying on "Judge Joe Brown."

To be fair, I did catch an archeological dig in Egypt, a bunch of people building a new home for a deserving family and some great insights into the styles of Pope John Paul II and Pope Benedict XVI by George Weigel.

What amazed me most is that such an amazing invention like TV can be so under-used to uplift and educate people, and instead be used to celebrate the worst side of human behavior. It did not occur to me for a minute to start a petition drive to clean up TV. I simply picked up the magic clicker and turned it off. Since TV is funded mostly through advertising, the most effective way to clean up TV is for enough people to simply turn it off.

February 9, 2006

34

Marriage, Priesthood have Lots of Similarities

Your light must shine before others, that they may see your good deeds and give glory to God because of them. Matthew 5: 16

You often hear people talk about marriage and priesthood as if they were opposites when, in fact, they are very similar.

The *Catechism of the Catholic Church* says that there are two sacraments directed toward the salvation of others: matrimony and holy orders. It goes on to say that "if marriage and ordination contribute to personal salvation, it is through service of others that they do so."

Simply put, couples get married and priests are ordained for others, for what they can do for others, not for what marriage and ordination can do for them. Our "light must shine for others." For me, others are the members of our church and beyond — everyone. For married couples, others are their spouses, their children, their families and their communities. We become holy and happy through our service to others.

God has filled us with his light. That light was not given to us for just our own good but for the good of other people. Our light must shine for the whole world to see; we must not clutch it to ourselves or hide it in some dark corner. Our light is meant to brighten the world. We must use all that has been given to us to enrich the lives of others, knowing that we will be enriched in the process.

We don't have to go far for models who have used their gifts and talents to enrich the lives of others and who have been enriched in the process. All we have to do is study the lives of couples who are still happily married after many years, as well as the lives of holy priests who are still happy and effective in their senior years.

What do married couples pledge — to feel warm and fuzzy about each other for the rest of their lives? No! That's Hollywood stuff. They pledge to be love-givers. In fact, they pledge to be love-givers regardless of what they get back, regardless of the circumstances, for the rest of their lives, starting with each other and expanding outward to the whole world.

If we focus on the love we give rather than the love we get, we will never be disappointed, because there will always be opportunities to love.

Weddings are fun, and marriages are hard work, just as ordinations are fun, and being an effective priest is hard work. As I ask our priests-to-be at the seminary, "Now that you will be a priest, what kind of priest do you will to be?" I ask young couples the same question, "Now that you will be married, what kind of marriage do you wish to have?"

"Living happily ever after" is not a matter of luck or magic, but of dedication, concentration and patience. A relationship is a living thing. It must be cared for and nurtured. We must "mind our calls."

February 16, 2006

Lent is about More than What We Eat

Change the way you see and believe in the Gospel. Mark 1:15

If you are one of those people who think Lent is only about giving up candy bars and filling a cardboard rice bowl with pennies, you've got another thought coming. Jesus might give us credit for meaning well, and it might be fine for small children, but he certainly expects more than that from us who are supposed to be adult Christians.

What Jesus wants from us is nothing less than our whole hearts, our whole souls and our whole strength, not trivial little religious games whereby we give up hot dogs, eat shrimp and think we are somehow doing God a great big favor. What Jesus wants from us is a radical change in the way we see things so that we are able to see God's love being played out right under our noses.

The first time I can remember consciously changing the way I looked at something took place two weeks after I was ordained. I had my heart set on being an associate pastor in Louisville where I could enjoy all that a big city had to offer. What I got was an assignment in the "home missions" as far away from Louisville as I could get. I was angry, but I had to go.

Halfway down there, around Danville, I had a dramatic conversion in my thinking. It was obvious to me that I could be there for as many as ten years, whether I was angry about it or not. I decided to change my mind, look at it with new eyes and embrace that assignment with all the good will and optimism that I could bring to it.

What I didn't know at the time was that it would turn out to be one of the greatest assignments of all. All I had to do was look at it differently.

Metanoiete! With these words of Jesus, we open another Lenten season. These words come to us after the devil proposed several tempting possibilities to Jesus about how he might approach his ministry. Basically, the devil suggested he change things. Jesus chose rather to call people to change.

Jesus did not fall for the devil's suggestion, because he knew that the only thing that needs to change is the way people see and think. Jesus knew that if people changed the way they see and think they would be able to see the goodness of God being played out, right under their very noses.

Things will change when people change. Things will change when people change the way they see, the way they think, the way they look at God and each other.

The message again this Lent is simple — things don't need changing nearly as much we do, because if we change, things will change for us. Lent is more about changing our thinking than it is our eating patterns.

February 23, 2006

Leadership is More than a Position and a Title

He taught them as one having authority and not as the scribes. Mark 1

One of the most painful lessons I had to learn as a priest was learned in my first year as pastor of the Cathedral. I had to learn that having the title of a leader did not necessarily mean that I was, in fact, a leader.

I had been given the title of "pastor of the Cathedral" with a young "associate pastor" to work with me. In many ways, I was in over my head. I had accepted the title of pastor, but I was somewhat ambivalent and unprepared for all that a pastor of an important and visible church such as the Cathedral needs to be. As a result of my indecision and lack of focus, the associate pastor "took charge" and left me in the dust.

Our constant clashes all came to a head one day when one of the musicians screamed out at a tense meeting, "The trouble around here is that we have two pastors." It hit me like a ton of bricks: I had the title and the associate had the power. Instead of being angry at him, I decided to step up to the plate and start acting like a pastor. It was a painful, but needed, growing experience.

Not everyone who holds a religious office or wears a robe is a spiritual leader. But you already know that from experience, don't you? You can spot a phony a mile away. You also know from experience the power of true spiritual leaders who are more than their office or the robes they wear. You know how attractive a real spiritual leader can be and how disappointing and destructive they can be when they are nothing more than "wolves in sheep's clothing."

I am worried about the growing gap between church leaders and our people. I do not believe that our people are resistant to being guided by authentic church teaching, but they do want real spiritual leaders under those mitres, behind those collars and underneath all those lay ministry titles.

But before you condemn too many religious leaders for being fakes and phonies, remember that you are also called to be religious leaders in your marriages, in your families, in your parishes and in your workplaces. Before you condemn your pastor or your bishop, you might evaluate your own spiritual leadership.

Many of you have accepted the role of godparents. Is there any gap between how you are supposed to act as role model for your godchild and the way you actually live?

Many of you hold the title of "parent," and as such, you are your children's primary faith teachers. Do you live what you teach? Do you even teach?

Most of my readers are "Catholics." What kind of example are you settling for the non-Catholics of this community? If people were to judge all Catholics by your behavior, how would we all be judged?

March 2, 2006

Little Questions are Important, Too

How inscrutable are your judgments and how unsearchable his ways! Romans 11:33

I have always marched to a different drummer, just a little out of step with the majority.

Seldom do the political candidates I vote for ever get elected. Priesthood is certainly not at the top of the list of the most sought-out professions.

I am different in another important way. I don't sit around asking the big questions, such as "why does God allow so much suffering?" or "why do some people find it easy to believe and others find it impossible?"

What I want to know is much more immediate and mundane.

I want to know why any sane man would wear a "pork-pie" hat, buy half-glasses for the end of his nose and hang them on a chain around his neck or why any grown man would wear a Disney "Goofy" sweatshirt in public.

I want to know why some women in a check-out line will not begin to dig though their huge purses for their checkbooks, much less begin to fill them out, until after the cashier has announced the total.

I want to know why some people in the left lane at a stoplight in an intersection will not turn on their turn signals until after the light changes. I want to know why golf is so obnoxiously addictive.

I want to know what people have to talk about that requires all that talking on cell phones. I want to know why anybody would buy a Scion, Aztec or PT Cruiser. I want to know why people park their grocery carts in the middle of the aisle and then go off and leave them there until you track them down and frown menacingly at them.

I want to know why stores that cover several city blocks never seem to have more than two check-out lanes open. I want to know why service personnel say, "I'll be right back," but never return. I want to know why one famous hamburger place seems to have a dozen people behind the counter while nobody seems to be concerned that lines of people are waiting to be served by two very confused counter people.

I want to know where parents get the patience to raise children. I want to know how teachers do it, standing in front of that much energy all day while trying to get it to go in a positive direction. I want to know how long-term health care givers to elderly parents or sick children keep going.

I want to know why Catholics who haven't darkened the doors of a church for years are the most demanding when it comes to weddings. I want to know why 90 percent of all the funerals I do fall on my day off no matter what day I pick.

I don't ask the big question because it is not the mountain ahead of me that wears me out; it is the small rocks in my shoe.

March 9, 2006

Peer Pressure isn't Just a Problem for Youth

It is you who must choose. Job 34:33

Peer pressure comes from an individual's need to have the acceptance and approval of his or her equals. It is a behavior pattern that begins in childhood and continues into adulthood. We tend to associate peer pressure with adolescence, but even well-adjusted adults often feel pressure to measure up to the expectations of their peers.

Even adults conform to what they believe to be the norms of the group in order to be accepted. We join groups of like-minded people in clubs and support groups to avoid the feelings and retribution for being "different." Non-conformists are punished, even while being secretly admired, in societies like ours. People are often threatened by being different at home, but on vacation, being different is actually sought out.

Some time ago I decided not to follow the crowd and to be my own person regardless of the reaction, something I could not have done without years of working on my self-esteem. Thinking about that, I decided to come up with a list of liberating things I choose to do, regardless of the reaction, acceptance or approval of others.

Several years ago my sisters and brothers decided to say "no" to the insane practice of buying unneeded gifts for each other at Christmas. We get together every year, as we did again this past Christmas, to enjoy a nice meal and each other's company, period! It is so much fun and so stress-free that I recommend it to other families.

We priests are asked to make our funeral plans, file them at the Chancery and update them regularly. I have decided to say "no" to the wasteful funeral practices of expensive caskets and monuments. I have chosen a "monk casket," an unfinished poplar box from Abbey

Caskets of Saint Meinrad Archabbey. I will be dressed in clothes I already own, and my marker will be deliberately minimal.

I have done many weddings in my life, but my favorites have been those who said "no" to the wasteful American wedding industry. I have seen some very beautiful, spiritual and simple weddings. In fact, the most spiritual have been the most simple, and the least spiritual have been the most gaudy and wasteful.

I give to organized charities like everyone else and receive my tax-deductible receipts. But I like even more to do random acts of generosity to individuals who need it but don't expect it, and for which there are no charitable deductions.

I like to say "no" to accumulation of too many material things. I go through my house at least once a year and get rid of stuff I don't need and don't use. I shop when I need something, not when I feel lonely or bored or for recreation. I like to own things I need and find useful. I hate it when my things start to own me.

Choose differently! It is freeing, if you are confident in yourself and not addicted to other people's opinions.

March 16, 2006

Speaking About God, not "For" God

Your mother and your brothers and sisters are
outside looking for you. Mark 3

Unlike the evangelists who came after him, the writer of Mark's
Gospel has an uncanny way of laying things out for you, unvarnished.
As respect and reverence for the apostles rose in the early church,
we find some of the stories in his Gospel "cleaned up" in the Gospels
that came later.

We see this in the story about the ambitions of James and John.
Mark says that the request for the best seats in Jesus' new kingdom
came out of the mouths of James and John. When Matthew tells the
same story later, this tacky request comes out of the mouth of their
mother. It's an old, and often useful, trick in ministry — to blame women.

We see this again in today's story about the family of Jesus show-
ing up to see him. Both Matthew and Luke record the story, but with
one big difference. Mark and Matthew both tell us that Jesus' family
showed up looking for a chance to speak with him, but only Mark tells
us why they wanted to see Jesus.

In a few verses preceding today's reading, we are told that his family "set out to seize Jesus because they said he was out of his mind."
They were convinced that he had "lost it," and they wanted to take
him home for his own good.

Ever since Adam and Eve there has been a tendency among hu-
mans to believe that they know better than God himself what needs
to be done. In prayer, instead of asking God to change us so that we
will do his will, we often attempt to use prayer as a way to bribe God
to do our will. It is like the funny prayer I saw recently that says, "Use
me Lord! Use me! Use me in some advisory capacity."

One warning to those of you who are clergy or pastoral workers: There have been many before us who started off speaking about God, but gradually moved toward speaking for God. After that, it is a short step to speaking as if you are God. From there, it is easy to think that even God is "out of his mind" and needs our advice.

Beware of preachers and politicians who are more than willing to clean up things for God. Ann Coulter says about the Middle East, "We ought to invade their countries, kill their leaders and convert them to Christianity." Jerry Falwell says, "The idea that religion and politics don't mix was invented by the devil to keep Christians from running their own country." Pat Robertson says that Ariel Sharon's stroke was inflicted by God as punishment. Jimmy Swaggart says, "If I don't return to the pulpit this weekend, millions of people will go to hell."

There may be no people more dangerous than the self-righteous who speak for God, because sooner or later they begin to believe they are God.

March 23, 2006

It's About What We Don't Do

Teacher, all of these I have observed from my youth. Mark 10:17-27

Before Catholics stopped going to weekly confession in great numbers, we used to hear confessions for at least an hour every day in one parish where I served. It was the place where people came to be deliberately anonymous.

Most of those confessions would put you to sleep; some would move you to tears and a few would spontaneously curl the hair on your head. The penitents who would irritate were not those who returned week after week having done the same old thing over and over, but the ones who confessed this way: "Bless me, Father, I don't know what to tell you. I didn't take the name of the Lord in vain. I didn't gossip. I didn't miss Sunday Mass. I didn't commit adultery. I didn't steal anything. My parents are dead, so I didn't disobey or disrespect them."

What was irritating was their belief that sin is only about doing bad things, and so their discipleship was reduced to simply avoiding bad things. They were like the rich young man who was able to say to Jesus, "I have observed all these commandments since my youth. I never did this! I never did that! I never did such and such!"

Unlike sinful me, Jesus did not get irritated by this young man's confidence in his ability not to break the commandments. It says that Jesus "looked at him with love." But after the kind smile, Jesus hit him between the eyes with a challenge: "Yes, you have avoided evil and that is good, but now do something great, do something positive, do something heroic. Let go of the thing you trust the most — your financial security — and trust me instead."

It says that "his face fell," and he "went away sad" because he couldn't "let go" of his "many possessions." He could avoid the bad thing, but he couldn't do the great thing.

The "Confiteor" is part of an ancient penitential rite in the Mass. It is an option that is regaining popularity, especially among young seminarians. It is still used in many places on a regular basis. In the Confiteor, we confess the bad we have done as well as the good that we have left undone. Very often we do not perpetuate horrible evils on each other nearly as much as we fail to do great things.

Maybe Edmund Burke summarized our sin best when he said, "All that is necessary for the triumph of evil is for enough good people to do nothing." Maybe the real problem of our church and world is not the handful of infamous evil people doing dreadfully bad things, nearly as much as the hordes of ordinary good people doing nothing great.

There is a lot more to Christianity than keeping our own noses clean. We probably sin more in the area of "what we have failed to do" than "what we have done."

March 30, 2006

Negative Thinking will Kill What Is Possible

No one pours new wine into old wineskins.
New wine is poured into fresh wineskins.
Mark 2

One of my heroes is Philo T. Farnsworth. I have a framed quote of his hanging on a very visible wall in my house. It says, "Impossible things just take a little longer."

If you don't recognize his name, you should. He is credited with inventing television. He believed that with an open mind anything was possible. Look how far television, once labeled "impossible," has come.

The reason Philo T. Farnsworth is a hero of mine is that I, too, believe that more things are possible than we can ever imagine. The realization of the impossible begins with an open mind. When I have consciously and deliberately kept my mind open, I have seen this dynamic unfold more times than I can count.

Negative thinking kills the possible. Here are a couple of examples from real life.

A shoe factory once sent two marketing scouts to a region of Africa to study the prospects for expanding the shoe business. One sent back a telegram that said, "Situation hopeless. No one wears shoes." The other sent back a telegram saying, "Great business opportunity. They have no shoes."

Thomas Watson, chairman of IBM, responded negatively to the idea of investing in computers in 1943 by saying, "I think there is a world market for maybe five computers." As late as 1977, Ken Olson, president, chairman and founder of Digital Equipment Corporation, said, "There is no reason anyone would want a computer in his home."

As a child, if I had not decided to reject it, I would have been a victim of this kind of negative thinking. Several significant adults in my life told me that I had no chance at all of making it through the seminary. I was even called a "hopeless case" by one seminary rector.

Because of these experiences, I stay in a mild state of irritation at our church when it seems unable to take advantage of the many opportunities staring it in the face even now. No wonder we have a vocation crisis. No wonder we are closing parishes. We are hopelessly mired in downward spiraling talk about both issues. Where are the can-do people who can see an alternative to our hopeless resignation?

Jesus tells us that God needs an open mind, a "new wineskin," to do his work of making all things new. Mary understood this when she said "yes" to God. She knew that when an open mind cooperates with God, then "all things are possible."

I pray for this kind of mind and heart. My prayer for this kind of mind and heart can be summed up in the words of Soren Kierkegaard when he said, "If I were to wish for anything I should not wish for wealth and power, but for the passionate sense of what can be, for the eye, which, ever young and ardent, sees the possible."

Faith can move mountains.

April 6, 2006

We All Have Our Roles
in Christ's Ministry

The Lord called Samuel. Samuel answered.
The Lord was with Samuel, not permitting any
word of his to be without effect. 1 Samuel 3

In January, I spent a week at Lake Barkley with Bishop McRaith and the priests of the Owensboro Diocese. That diocese was the first of several dioceses around the country that agreed to hold a week-long retreat that I developed. The retreat is designed to help priests work closer together as a team so they can offer better service to you.

Believe it or not, 90 percent of all priests are happy being priests, even though we have been though some pretty traumatic events in the last few years that have left many of us a little disoriented and confused about where to go from here.

Our numbers are dropping, and our workloads are expanding. In a very real sense, all of us are being punished along with the guilty. This unhealthy dynamic, I believe, could lead to all the problems that manifest themselves in the lives of people under too much pressure: over eating, over drinking, depression, acting out inappropriately and maybe even giving it up altogether.

Part of my agenda in designing this week-long retreat was this: Since we priests can't work much harder, we must learn to work smarter. And the best way to work smarter is to work more as a team.

Another part of my agenda is to remind priests who they are, why they do what they do and how to recover some of their original enthusiasm.

In light of that experience and the fact that today is Holy Thursday when we celebrate the priesthood, I thought I would take this opportunity to talk about some basics of the relationships between priests and those they serve. Sometimes it is good to go back to the basics so we can remember the fundamentals.

Our lives as priests don't make sense apart from you. Diocesan priests are called from the laity, to live among the laity, so as to empower the laity in living out their Christian discipleship. We serve you in three basic ways: we are preachers of the Gospel, we preside at the celebration of the sacraments and we lead communities of faith.

Through baptism all of us, men and women, share in carrying out some part of Christ's ministry. Out of all those who make up this "common priesthood," some of us were called to serve the community in "ordained ministry." We exist to help you. That is who we are in relationship to you. We cannot forget that, and you must not let us forget that essential fact.

Because we are called to serve you, our health or lack of it has a direct impact on you. Pray for your priests.

Last of all, remember that regardless of how well we do our jobs or how badly we do them, you are still called to carry on your share of Christ's ministry in building up his church.

April 13, 2006

Though not Perfect, Some Parishes are Close

The community of believers were of one heart and one mind. Acts 4:32

After Easter, we have some beautiful snapshots of the early church. Some of them are idealized, no doubt, but they give us an ideal to reach for nonetheless. One of those snapshots pictures the church as being of "one mind and one heart."

I am sure there were great days when it seemed that the church was of "one heart and one mind," but if you keep reading you realize that the whole story is that it was a mixture of highs like this and also some lows as well. Not too much later in the same book of Scripture, we read that Paul and Barnabas had to go their separate ways after a major disagreement. Now that sounds more familiar.

There are no perfect parishes, but some come close to the ideal. I have just returned from preaching a parish mission in Grove City, Fla., in the Diocese of Venice. The response was better than I could have imagined. I am still moved by all that I experienced there. It was my second series of talks in that parish, but my third in the Diocese of Venice. I gave a parish mission at its Cathedral of the Nativity a few years back.

Carmelite Father Bart Larkin, formerly of DeSales High School and Our Lady of Mount Carmel parish in Louisville, is the pastor. He is a loved pastor. It is obvious in the eyes and voices of his parishioners. I thought of Father Andrew Greeley's words, "When a priest is in a parish he loves and is loved by his parishioners, he is like a man in love."

Father Bart is assisted by Father Marcel, another good Carmelite, as well as Sisters Eileen and Monica, who are still working well beyond the ages when most of the people they serve have retired. There also is a diverse staff of capable staff members and volunteers, including Midge Swartz, who handles the selling of my books.

The parish is made up mostly of retired people from the north and northeastern states. During the winter months "regular visitors" fill the church. From what I heard, their worries fall into three main categories: their kids, their health and their golf games, but not necessarily in that order.

They are from that generation of most faithful Catholics who have loved their church and their priests through thick and thin. They know how to pray and, thanks to Bill Strain, I have never heard such good congregational singing in my life. They exude a basic goodness that I find irresistible.

I think I have been invited to go back to a neighboring parish for an Advent parish mission. If I play my cards right, I may have an "in" when I retire. It would be nice to be able to volunteer there a couple of months each winter and help out in Louisville the rest of the time.

April 20, 2006

Most Lies are Attempts to Boost Our Egos

The truth will set you free. John 8:32

Do you lie? If you said "no," you are probably lying. Lies can be as harmless as exaggerating the size of the fish you caught and as destructive as lying under oath in a murder trial. Most of us probably fall somewhere in the middle.

Why do we lie? Most of our lies are pitiful attempts to bolster our egos. We lie because we fear being shamed or embarrassed if we do not measure up. One country song challenges such efforts when it says, "I'd rather be hated for who I am than be loved for what I'm not!" Arthur Calwell offers some similar advice when he says, "It is better to be defeated on principle than to win on lies."

We lie because we do not want to do something, whether paying more for something or doing more work. We lie when we have already done wrong, know it and are ashamed of our own behavior. We lie when we believe that it is justified to accomplish our urgent goals. This happens in politics, commerce and even in the church when people lie to reach their goals. We lie when we hold back part of the whole truth or when we subtly mislead.

Maybe the worst kind of lying is the lying we do to ourselves so that we can live with the violations of our own conscience. Alcohol and drugs are often used to help us numb ourselves against that "small voice that sounds in our ears that tells us the right way to go" that Isaiah (30:21) speaks about.

It is a small step from lying to ourselves to lying to others. Shakespeare was right when he wrote: "This above all — to thine own self be true. And it must follow as night the day, thou canst not then be false to any man."

Most of us take lying for granted. We expect it. Some can actually spot it more quickly than others. Their alarm bells go off in the middle of commercials, election ads and so-called "no spin" talk shows. A few fall for anything they hear. Otto Von Bismarck may have summed up best our cynicism about being told the truth when he said, "People never lie so much as after a hunt, during a war or before an election."

Lying is actually hard work and requires a great memory. Sir Walter Scott had something to say about the former when he wrote, "Oh, what a tangled web we weave, when first we practice to deceive." Mark Twain had something great to say about the latter when he wrote: "Always tell the truth. That way, you don't have to remember what you said."

Christians must put away lying and all its spin-offs — deceit, guile, duplicity and exaggeration. Instead, we must be committed to living in the truth, knowing that ultimately "the truth will set us free" even if it is inconvenient in the short run.

April 27, 2006

Losing a Life in order to Save the World

Unless a grain of wheat falls to the ground
and dies, it remains just a grain of wheat, but if
it dies, it produces much fruit. John 12

I have one single grain of wheat in a small vial on my desk to remind me of the message of Easter. I could preserve this grain in this air-tight container for years and years and keep it indefinitely. On the other hand, I could plant this single grain of wheat, and, given enough time, I could literally feed the world.

If I were to bury this one single grain in the earth, in a few weeks it would give itself to become a sprout, then a shoot, then a stalk and finally 50 or more new grains of wheat.

Those 50 or more grains, buried in the ground, would soon become 2,500 or more grains.

Those 2,500 or more grains, buried in the ground, would in turn become 125,000 or more grains.

Each time I would do that, the number of grains would expand at a faster and faster rate, even if some were lost to animals, disease or weather. In time, this single grain of wheat could theoretically produce enough wheat to feed the whole world!

Jesus was simply using the image of a grain of wheat, giving its life to produce millions more grains of wheat, to talk about his own death and resurrection. A grain of wheat is ineffective and unfruitful as long as it is preserved in safety and security, and it only bears fruit when it is thrown into the cold ground and buried, as in a tomb. So it was with the death of Jesus.

His death on the cross and burial in the earth would lead to his resurrection and new life for millions upon millions of his followers — indeed, for all humankind.

This did not just happen once with the historic death and resurrection of Jesus. This is a basic life principle. "Whoever tries to save his life will lose it, and whoever loses his life for my sake will save it." "Life coming through death" is life's biggest paradox.

This process can be accepted or initiated. Often life brings us unexpected or unwanted changes, changes that take us into new places, welcomed or not. Sometimes we get up the courage to initiate a crisis to set the process in motion: we leave crippling relationships, sign ourselves into a treatment and quit jobs that are killing us.

In a way, we "bury" our old life in the belief that it is the path to a new one. The secret is to embrace the dying and rising process, trusting that it will bring us the new life we need and want.

If we live this mystery — dying and rising over and over again — when we get to the end of our earthly lives, we can even embrace our own death, knowing that this life will simply be traded in for a life that we cannot begin to imagine.

May 4, 2006

It's the Message, not the Messenger

Gods have come to us in the form of men.
Acts 14

Next Tuesday, I will celebrate my 36th anniversary as a priest. It is hard for me to believe, but "time goes by when you're having fun."

Each anniversary I like to take a little time to reflect on the journey that has led me to this point and to pray for the strength that I will need to keep going.

Mostly I am amazed and grateful. I am not only amazed that I made it through the seminary, I am also amazed that I am left standing when most of the guys I went to the seminary with did not make it. I am amazed that I am still a priest when half of my ordination class members are no longer in the priesthood.

I am not only amazed, I am grateful. I am grateful that I have not only survived in the priesthood for 36 years, I have thrived in the priest-hood. I am among the 90-plus percent of priests today who are happy being priests and would choose it again.

Many things have changed in these last 36 years. One big thing that has changed is the disappearance of the pedestal that people used to put priests on — something that lay people have seemed to want to do to their priests from the very beginning.

Some priests enjoyed the pedestal days. Some priests even want to bring them back.

I believe that the priesthood ought to be respected, but personally I think pedestals are dangerous places for priests to stand. When people put priests on pedestals, they run the risk of mistaking the messenger for the message. When priests let themselves be placed on a pedestal, it is a perfect set-up for disappointment. I believe it is best to remember that the validity of the message is always more important than the personal goodness of the messenger.

We see this confusion of the message with the messenger in the reading cited above. After Paul and Barnabas had healed the cripple in Lystra, the people wanted to start worshipping them. Mistaking them for gods, Paul and Barnabas could scarcely stop the people from worshipping them.

Fifteen hundred years ago St. John Chrysostom decried the need of people to put priests on pedestals when he wrote, "Everyone wants to judge the priest, not as one clothed in flesh, not possessing of a human nature, but as an angel, exempt from the frailty of others."

I agree with retired Archbishop John Quinn, who said that this is a great time to be a priest — not the easiest time, but certainly a great time. Motives are being purified. Most of the perks and pedestals are gone. Respect has to be earned. There really isn't any reason to be a priest anymore, except to serve. That, I believe, is a healthy place for a priest to be.

May 11, 2006

Foreign-Born Priests not New to the Church

They were all filled with the Holy Spirit and began to speak in different tongues, as the Spirit enabled them to proclaim. Acts 2:4

As the director of Saint Meinrad's new Institute for Priests and Presbyterates, one of my jobs is to teach a pastoral leadership class, with special emphasis on making the transition from seminary into priesthood for those about to be ordained. I love my job in general, but this part of it in particular.

This year's class was made up of seminarians from the dioceses of Dubuque, Davenport, Green Bay, Peoria, Evansville, Phoenix, Toledo, Louisville, Indianapolis, Crookston and Fresno, as well as a Trappist from New York and a Benedictine from New Mexico. Of these, one is from Vietnam, one from Korea, one from El Salvador and one from Columbia. Other students studying at Saint Meinrad this past year were from India, Mexico, the Philippines and Togo in Africa.

The percentage of foreign-born seminarians in seminaries, and priests in dioceses, is now typical across the country -- 28 percent and growing. Some might assume that this is something new. Not so! It is simply history repeating itself.

According to a new study by Dean Hoge and Aniedi Okure, the Catholic church in the United States has always had international priests serving its parishes, and in most of its history it has depended on them. Until the end of the 19th century, foreign-born priests — mainly from Ireland, France and Germany — dominated the church in America.

The early Catholic communities in the United States produced very few native-born priests. The American bishops needed to look to Europe, and they did so at every chance. They wrote to their friends and sent recruiters.

In 1791, at the first church synod held in Baltimore, 80 percent of the clergy present were foreign-born — French priests being the most common. At the second plenary council in Baltimore in 1866, 30 of the 47 bishops were foreign-born.

There were two complaints about priests from Europe in those days. First, they tended not to understand the separation of church and state and preferred a more hierarchical style of church than what they found here.

Second, the American church accepted almost any priest, only to find out later that many of them were misfits and malcontents back home. We had become the dumping ground for clergy of the lowest quality. Many toughed it out, and some returned home.

It was not until the 1940s and 1950s that the chronic American priest shortage eased. This period, contrary to what many Catholics today think, was an exception to the rule. The longer-term American picture is one of a shortage of American seminarians and an endless effort to recruit priests from overseas.

Unlike the past, today's foreign-born seminarians are often the cream of the crop. They are screened well, and most have a facility for learning more than one language. Like they did the past, foreign-born priests follow immigration patterns.

"The more things change, the more they stay the same."

May 18, 2006

A Tribute to the "Innocent Majority" of Priests

And every day the Lord added to their number those who were being saved. Acts 2:47

Maybe you missed it, sandwiched in between the relentless bad news, but there was a big piece of good news about the Catholic church last month. A total of 68,016 adults freely joined the Catholic church either as new Christians through baptism or as new Catholics through profession of faith — 587 of them here in our own diocese.

After all we have been through, I find that amazing.

This good news made me look forward to the day when we Catholics begin to recover from the shame that has infected the church these last few years and start doing the great things we have always done as a church and openly celebrating the goodness that is within us.

This good news made me realize once again that I am proud to be Catholic, even though I have been selective in where I express my feelings. The last time I had these feelings was during the funeral of Pope John Paul II.

One of the ways I have tried to cope and keep my head up during this period of darkness, sadness and disorientation was to express my feelings through writing. This column is a tangible expression of trying to get my feelings out rather than have them eat me alive by holding them in. Writing this column may have helped others, but I believe it may have helped me even more.

Another way I have tried to cope with this period of darkness, sadness and disorientation was to write two books directed at today's priests and seminarians. The innocent majority have been shamed as they watched their profession, once thought of as an admirable if not heroic profession, disgraced before the whole world.

My "Intentional Presbyterates" is now being studied all over the country as priests move through this nightmare and try to find glimmers of hope as they continue their ministry. I am seeing priests in one diocese after the other beginning to lift their heads, pull themselves together and move on.

My "From Seminarian to Diocesan Priest" talks young priests through some of the hidden dynamics and unseen fallout that will face them as they leave the security of the seminary and move into a priesthood that will continue to be marked by the residue of those dark days. It is my "encouraging word" to them.

Yes, I am ready to be openly proud to be Catholic again. I am looking for reasons to hope, and each day I am seeing what I have been looking for — great things such as the influx of thousands of new members who can see beyond our sins to the incredible goodness that is the church around the world even today.

Finally, I am even more ready to see talented and generous young men begin to respond once again to God's call to serve the church as priests — one of the most rewarding and life-giving of all the "calls."

May 25, 2006

Perhaps Old Dogs can Learn New Tricks

The age that is honorable cannot be measured in terms of years. Wisdom 4:8

I just turned 62. For other people, 62 doesn't sound all that old. Applied to me it certainly does. Unless my upcoming physical reveals something horrible, I seem to be in good health.

Though many of my friends, some even younger, are beginning to retire, I am very aware that I have eight more years to go. Because of the priest shortage, I am also braced for the fact that our next bishop may want to move the retirement age from 70 to 75 or even higher.

Even at that, it is beginning to occur to me that, if there is something more I want to do before I die, now is the time to get busy doing it. To override the natural tendency of thinking that the best is behind me, I keep a small pillow on my bed that helps me challenge that kind of thinking. In needlepoint it says: "The best is yet to come."

We need to challenge the thinking that we all do about aging. "I'm too old" is something we tell ourselves to save ourselves from the embarrassment of being a beginner. "I'm too old" is an evasive tactic. So is "I'm too young." They are both always used to avoid facing fear. As Charles Lamb put it, "We grow gray in spirit long before we grow gray in our hair."

Eleanor Roosevelt said, "I could not, at any age, be content to take my place in a corner by the fireplace and simply look on."

The first enemy we have to challenge, if we are to do things we have never done, is to face the enemy within. Otherwise, we will find ourselves standing on the sideline of a longed-for activity.

Aging may be more about attitude than marking a number of years. Mark Twain made a good point when he said, "Age is an issue of mind over matter. If you don't mind, it doesn't matter." Samuel Ullman put it this way: "Nobody grows old merely by living a number of years. We grow old by deserting our ideals. Age may wrinkle the skin, but to give up enthusiasm wrinkles the soul." John Barrymore said, "A man is not old until regrets take the place of dreams."

I would not want to go back, even if I could. There are at least as many advantages to being 62 as there were to being 32 and maybe more. Henry Wadsworth Longfellow spoke of the trade-off when he said, "Age is opportunity no less than youth itself, though in another dress. And as the evening twilight fades away, the sky is filled with stars, invisible by day."

On second thought, maybe the 60s are the most demanding years of all. As T.S. Eliot put it, "The years between 50 and 70 are the hardest. You are always being asked to do more, and you are not yet decrepit enough to turn them down."

June 1, 2006

Blessed is the Man who has a Brother

How good and how pleasant it is for brothers
to dwell in unity. Psalm 133:1

I have two brothers, Gary and Mark. Mark's birthday was June 2; Gary's birthday is today. In honor of both of them, I have declared today "brothers day."

My brother Gary is more like my grandfather, Leo. He has the ability to sit and watch a fishing pole for hours on end. Just as my grandfather was, Gary is laid back, patient and generous — probably too generous sometimes. And just as my mother did, he tends to put the needs of others before his own.

My brother Mark and I, on the other hand, are more like my Dad — passionately driven to accomplish our goals, sometimes to the point of personal exhaustion and to the aggravation of others. We like to see just how far we can go. Having no new projects to obsess about is our enemy.

Both brothers have carried on the Knott tradition of working in lumber. Gary has been successful in buying and cutting timber, some-thing that both my Granddad and Dad did in turn. (I will not mention the fact that he has "retired" at least twice and is now back to work.) Mark has done an amazing job of expanding my Dad's building mate-rial business. I even inherited a mild form of the "disease" by remodel-ing a total of six houses so far.

Garrison Keeler may have touched on our relationships when we were kids when he said, "The highlight of my childhood was making my brother laugh so hard that food came out his nose." Thankfully, it has progressed from there.

Catherine Pulsifer may have described our relationship best when she said, "As we grew up, my brothers acted like they didn't care, but

I always knew they looked out for me and were there." As we have gotten older our relationship as brothers has outlasted marriages, survived the death of parents and resurfaced after a few less-than-serious quarrels. We even still laugh about things such as "the time we laughed so hard food came out his nose."

One of the best things we ever did together as brothers was to host an annual "Uncle Party" for several years for our 20 young nieces and nephews. They are still talking about it.

Blessed is the man who has a brother. Blessed even more is the one who has two. Maybe the words of St. Francis of Assisi could be applied to those of us who are lucky enough to have brothers. "Blessed is the servant who loves his brother as much when he is sick and useless as when he is well and can be of service to him, and blessed is he who loves his brother as well when he is afar off as when he is by his side and who would say nothing behind his back he might not, in love, say before his face."

Gary and Mark, happy "brothers day!" Know your brother loves you both.

June 8, 2006

Avoiding the Near Occasion of Sin

And do not put us to the test. Luke 11:4

During my sabbatical, I lost quite a bit of weight. During a one-month period, I ate very little and walked the beach for five hours a day. I lost about five inches in my waist. Following the advice of the weight-loss gurus, I got rid of my old clothes so that I would not be tempted to grow into them again. Ha! What a joke! I have been buying them back, one pair of pants at a time, over the last two years.

It seems that I have fallen for Oscar Wilde's advice when he said, "The best way to get rid of temptation is to give into it." I was feeling like those "victims" on the "Maury Povich Show" who do all kinds of awful things and the only excuse they can come up with is, "It was there."

What could I do?" Even Buddha knew better when he said, "It is a man's own mind, not his enemy or foe, that lures him into evil ways."

I would love to blame Saint Meinrad.

Here in Louisville, I deal with the temptation to overeat by not having food in the house. At Saint Meinrad, I am faced with a buffet three times a day. Unfortunately, their bakery is superb. What human being could resist those big trays of homemade doughnuts every Tuesday morning? I agree with Homer Simpson when he said, "Ah, doughnuts! Is there anything they can't do?" I hate myself when I start agreeing with Oscar Wilde when he said, "I can resist anything but temptation."

Henry Ward Beecher said, "All men are tempted. There is no man that lives that can't be broken down, provided it is the right temptation, put in the right spot."

I find it horrifying to know that, under the right circumstances, most of us are capable of anything.

The solution, at least for me, not just with overeating, but with other sins as well, is controlling my circumstances and praying, "lead me not into temptation." Controlling one's circumstances and the ability to say "no" to oneself are keys to self-mastery.

"Controlling one's circumstances" is just another way of saying what priests and nuns of childhood days used to call "avoiding the near occasion of sin." A lot of people, even Catholics, like to laugh at that kind of teaching, but there is a lot of wisdom in many of the things they taught us. Even Alcoholics Anonymous teaches people about controlling their circumstances when they teach people not to return to their old drinking buddies and drinking spots.

Completely avoiding the "occasion of sin" is impossible, so developing the ability to say "no" is crucial. Self-discipline has at its root the ability to talk back to one's feelings. Sometimes we just have to stand up to ourselves and say "no" for our own good. God can help. I hope so, because I'm back on my diet.

June 15, 2006

There will be Great Reward for Care-Givers

When you were younger, you used to dress yourself and go where you wanted; but when you grow old, you will stretch out your hands, and someone else will dress you and lead you where you do not want to go. John 21:18

Where was my camera when I needed it? The other day I was standing on my deck looking out toward the street. There, on the steepest stretch of the sidewalk in front of my house, was a woman pushing an old man in a wheelchair. She was struggling, with her head down and body stretched out, to push him to the top where it was level again.

Right behind her, a few yards back, was another woman pushing a huge, loaded-down, baby stroller. She, too, was struggling, with her head down and her body stretched out to push the heavy stroller up the hill.

It occurred to me that at both ends of our lives we depend on people to help us, whether it be as helpless children or helpless old people. For one who is overly independent in his thinking, it made a chill come over me.

I've been that baby, and someday I will be that old man. I had someone to push my stroller, but will I have anyone to push my wheelchair? If I am lucky, I'll simply die in my sleep and never have to find out.

I still cannot get that scene off my mind. Maybe it is because I recently presided at the funeral of the husband of my cousin, Karen. She is in the advanced stages of MS and was totally dependent on him as her care-taker until he died suddenly of a heart attack. He was a good man and a faithful care-giver. His was one of the most tragic funerals in my life.

I am reminded of a quote from the Dalai Lama: "Right from the moment of our birth, we are under the care and kindness of our parents, and then later on in our life when we are oppressed by sickness and become old, we are again dependent on the kindness of others. Since at the beginning and the end of our lives we are so dependent on others' kindness, how can it be in the middle that we would neglect kindness toward others?"

Phyllis Diller said it more humorously. "Be nice to your children, for they will choose your rest home."

Today, in memory of Daryl, my cousin's husband, I want to offer "an encouraging word" to the more than 50 million people each year who provide care at home for the chronically ill, disabled or aged — 56 percent of them women, 44 percent men. Their average length of service is eight years. Most women will spend 17 years caring for children and 18 years helping an elderly parent.

Their reward in heaven will be great, "for as long as you did it for these, you did it for me."

June 22, 2006

The Bravery of the Newest Catholics

Decide today whom you will serve. Joshua 24:15

Let me offer a few more "encouraging words" to the 68,000 new Catholics in this country — including the 587 locally — who joined the church this past Easter. I have been thinking about their courage, and I want to hold it up one more time to all of us who have remained faithful to the church in a time of great change and stress.

Talk about swimming against the stream. Their bravery should make us proud.

I also have been thinking about those who, in perhaps even greater numbers, have left the church during this same time. Why would some join and others leave? Some no doubt see the glass as half full, while others see it as half empty.

I stand with those who see the glass as half-full. I know the church is *semper reformanda*, always needing reform. But fundamentally I do not see the church as just another flawed human institution meriting contempt, but as the scarred and bruised Body of Christ in need of healing.

What is wrong with our church is not so much the fault of those who failed or even those who threw their lot into the ring with the religious right who have been seduced by political power. More fault lies with those who have dropped out of the fight and stand outside the margins as self-righteous critics. Critics can be right about their assessments and wrong about what they choose to do about it.

I agree with Theodore Roosevelt, who said: "It is not the critic who counts: not the man who points out how the strong man stumbles, or where the doer of deeds could have done them better. The credit belongs to the man who is actually in the arena, whose face is marred by dust and sweat and blood: who strives valiantly, who errs, and comes up short again and again, because there is no effort without error or shortcoming; but who does actually strive to do the deeds; who knows the great enthusiasms, the great devotions; who spends himself in a worthy cause; who at best knows in the end the triumph of high achievement, and who at worst, if he fails, at least fails while daring greatly, so that his place shall never be with those cold and timid souls who know neither victory nor defeat."

This latest influx of new Catholics has reminded me once again that there is something beautiful, something attractive, something awesome about our church that transcends our weaknesses and failures. They remind me once again that we are not just the church of the great saints of old, such as Francis of Assisi and Theresa of Avila, but also the church of the great saints of late, such as Pope John Paul II and Mother Teresa.

Just as I encourage those who have joined us, I challenge those who have left us. Come home, not because the church is perfect, but because it isn't.

June 29, 2006

Thanks to the Sisters of Charity of Nazareth

We give you thanks, O God! Psalm 75:2

I recently presided at the funeral of my first- and second-grade teacher. I have known Sister Mary Ancilla all my life. She arrived at my parish, St. Theresa in Meade County, when I was one year old. We stayed in touch until her death. I went to the old St. Theresa Academy for the first grade and to the newer St. Theresa School for the second.

Yes, she taught me to read and write; she taught the catechism to me and taught me how to be an altar boy. But she taught me something even more important: She taught me to see that I had potential, and she encouraged me to develop it.

One special memory stands out. She encouraged me to enter a county-wide fire prevention poster contest. I was 6 years old: bashful, skinny, painfully shy and totally lacking in self-confidence. I drew two kids playing in a fireplace on one half of my poster and one of those kids in a bed, burned, on the other half. His mother stood by the bed with a spoonful of medicine and huge teardrops coming out of both eyes.

She called me to the convent parlor one Saturday to make some final touch-ups. I was honored beyond belief to be invited to the "holy of holies," the convent parlor, just little old me, all by myself, on a Saturday. Well, my poster won first prize, which was presented to me in front of the whole school.

I knew this good woman all my life, but she is only one of the Sisters of Charity of Nazareth I know and admire. Everything I can say about her could be said about most of them.

Even though many of them are old, some sick, and the numbers to carry on their work are few, know this: They have done great things for thousands of kids from the small towns of Kentucky, Maryland, Arkansas and several other states, not to mention India, Nepal and Botswana.

They saw potential underneath our simple lives and backward ways. They not only taught us to read and write, but also they encouraged us to grow into good, healthy, holy and happy people. So what if some of them were not perfect. Who is? They certainly did not have perfect students either.

If they ever wonder whether their lives were worth it, let me tell them today, in no uncertain terms, that they can go to their rests confident that they were. Some of us, unfortunately, have never taken the time to tell them thanks, but have settled into judging their whole lives by their worst days. Whether we thanked them or not, God knows, and that is all that counts in the end, anyway.

As I say good-bye to Sister Mary Ancilla, a truly important player in my life, I want to thank God again for the Sisters of Charity of Nazareth, indeed for all our religious communities of women.

July 6, 2006

Self-Professed "Christians" Sometimes Aren't

Those who say, "I know him," but do not keep
his commandments are liars. 1 John 2

St. John uses the word "liar" five times in this letter. It is used in this letter more than in any other book of the Bible. John is obviously determined that people should understand that Christianity is not simply a "head trip," a question only of knowledge. He insists that we must do what we profess: we must practice what we preach and live what we say we believe.

America is a place saturated in Christian identity, but are we really that "Christian" nation we hear so much about?

Jesus put the love of neighbor on the same par as the love of God and made it the very core of the Christian message, spelling out what "loving" one's neighbor means: feeding the hungry, clothing the naked, welcoming the stranger and visiting the prisoner. How well does this "Christian" nation actually do in this regard?

In 2004, we ranked second to last, after Italy, among developed countries in foreign aid. Eighteen percent of American children live in poverty, compared to eight percent in Sweden. In fact, when it comes to childhood nutrition, infant mortality and access to preschool, we come in last among the rich nations, and often by a wide margin. In all the categories that Jesus paid particular attention to, we trail badly.

This nation has a murder rate four or five times that of our European peers. We are the most violent rich nation on earth. We have prison populations six or seven times higher than any other rich nation. We are the only Western democracy that executes its citizens, mostly in those states where "Christianity" is theoretically strongest.

Despite Jesus' strong declaration against divorce, five out of ten marriages end in divorce, compared to four out of ten in Europe. We top the charts in teenage pregnancy. When it comes to self-discipline, we have an abysmal record when it comes to things such as weight control, credit debt and government deficits.

I love this country, and I would hope that it would be a "Christian" country, but truly Christian — a country that cares for the poor, the sick, the naked and the hungry; a country that respects all people regardless of race, religion, language or way of life; a country respected around the world for its living of Jesus' principle of love for all — yes, even one's enemies.

It seems that the loudest self-professed "Christians" of this country are inviting us to subvert the teachings of Jesus, even as we celebrate them. Yes, I want my country to be "Christian," but I refuse to buy into a 700 Club notion of what a "Christian" nation should look like. If being a "Christian" nation means every dog for himself, let the poor help themselves; if it means hatred for Jews and Muslims, blurring the lines between the separation of church and state and cozy, self-obsessed mega-churches, I want no part of it.

July 13, 2006

A Little Knowledge can be a Dangerous Thing

Saul, for his part, concurred in the act of killing. Acts 8:1

I love St. Peter, the big lug with a soft heart. He set high standards for himself but kept falling on his face when he tried to measure up. He bragged a lot but ended up having to eat many of his words. He wanted to carry through on his big claims, even when he couldn't. He knew he was weak, and he owned up to it. I like that about him. I can relate.

On the other hand, I have always found St. Paul hard to warm up to, especially as a seminarian and a young priest. I always put Paul on my "saints who make me nervous" list, along with John the Baptist. Paul has always seemed a little too cocksure, a little too certain, a little too clear about everything, both before and after his conversion.

As I have gotten older, I have warmed up to St. Paul a little more. I do admire his passionate nature. When he locks onto something, he gives it everything he's got. I share that with him. When I lock onto an idea that I believe in, I sometimes become so passionate about it that I find it very hard to let go.

I admire Paul's passion and zeal, but he also teaches me that passion and zeal alone are not enough. Proverbs 19:2 tells us that "without knowledge, even zeal is not good." This is the case in point with St. Paul. As Saul, he was so passionate about preserving the "old-time religion," the orthodoxy of the Jewish faith, that he was willing to kill.

Saul held the coats of those who stoned Stephen to death, no doubt thinking he was doing God and Judaism a favor by ridding it of the followers of "this new way." In fact, his conversion took place on his way to round up more of these "heretics" for extinction. Just because Saul thought he was doing God's will did not in fact mean he was.

One of the things I have learned from St. Paul is the same thing I learned from the aforementioned Proverbs 19:2 — "Without knowledge, even zeal is not good." This insight is also contained in the saying, "A little knowledge is a dangerous thing." This insight is important to those who are zealous about beginning ministry as well as for those of us who are zealous about continuing in ministry.

There is nothing more dangerous in the church than this unholy mixture of arrogance and ignorance. Ideologues on the far left and far right are becoming more rigid in defending their half-truths. This is turning a "catholic" church into a loose association of warring tribes, pitting parish against parish, parishioner against parishioner and priest against priest. This is a sin.

We need Pope Paul's VI's "asceticism of dialogue," a fancy way of saying we need to learn how to talk to, and about, each other with respect.

July 20, 2006

What it Means to be a "Good" Shepherd

I am the good shepherd. John 10:11

A few years back I was watching a TV program about sheep dogs in Australia while at the same time working on a homily about the reading on the Good Shepherd. It dawned on me then, and I have never forgotten it, that there are at least two very different ways to herd sheep.

One way is to walk in front of them, gently calling to them while they follow behind, leading them to where they need to go. The other way is to bark and snap from behind, chasing and intimidating them into going where they need to go.

This is an important insight that I like to use in my class at Saint Meinrad for those who are about to become shepherds of God's people as pastors in the church. I try to inspire them individually to become a convincing presence so that people will want to go in the right way. And I warn them not to attempt barking and snapping at their parishioners in hopes of herding them in the right direction.

Jesus is the model for all in leadership, whether he is the model for baptismal priests or ordained priests. Jesus called himself the "good" shepherd. It is important to understand what he meant by "good."

There are two words for "good" in Greek: agathos and kalos. Agathos means good as in a "good person." Kalos means good as in a "good dancer." Agathos is about moral status. Kalos is about ability. Of course, Jesus is a morally good shepherd, but he is also a shepherd who is good at shepherding.

Because of our baptisms, all are called to "act in the person of Christ." We are all called to be "good" shepherds, capable of leading those entrusted to our care. This is especially true for parents, service professionals, spouses, teachers and those of us in ordained or lay ministry.

Parents must be good people, but also good at parenting. Teachers must be good people, but also good at teaching. Spouses must be good people, but also good at being a partner. Lay ministers, just as ordained ministers, must be good people, but they must also be good at ministry.

I have been doing a lot of reading on the topic of spiritual leadership in preparation for writing my next book on that subject for seminarians. The spiritual leader's task is to move people from where they are to where God wants them to be. Moving people is not the same thing as driving or forcing people to do something. It is a process of persuasion and example.

Parents, teachers and pastors often turn into sheep dogs when they fail at being good shepherds. Lacking the ability to gain the trust and to influence those they lead, they resort to angry barking, snapping and condemning. If spiritual leaders have to demand that they be listened to, they no longer lead spiritually, whether they are parents, religion teachers or priests.

July 27, 2006

Dealing with the Storms of Life

A violent squall came up, and waves were breaking over the boat. Jesus was asleep on a cushion. Mark 4

Have you ever been so scared, so panic-stricken, so overwhelmed with terror that you thought you'd die? Sadly, there are people in this world who live, year in and year out, in sheer terror of losing their lives through violence, grinding poverty or disease.

The passengers on the plane that went down in Pennsylvania on 9/11 were forced to leave this world in a heightened, panic-stricken state. Some terrorists even enjoy watching their victims suspended in a state of panic and terror. It must be a human being's worst nightmare to know clearly that he or she is going to die in a few seconds without the means to stop it.

Most people naturally turn to God in such moments. As the old saying goes, "There are no atheists in foxholes!"

Mark describes such a situation in today's Gospel. Every detail of the story is important. It was evening when they got into a small fishing boat to set sail across open water. A violent squall came up, and waves starting breaking over the boat, causing it to start sinking. Jesus was sleeping. They woke him, and he quieted the seas and their panicked hearts.

Imagine being in a sinking boat, on a lake, in a storm, after dark. Fear of drowning is terrifying. I know. When I was a teenager, I watched one of my closest friends drown. To this day, I can still see the panic in his eyes as he went down a final time.

Mark's story was, no doubt, based on an actual event, but the fact that it happened is not as important as why the early church put it into its Scriptures. The early church, persecuted for its faith, saw itself besieged by storms, while the resurrected and ascended Jesus seemed to be indifferent and absent from their problems. But they also knew that when they turned to him in prayer and trust, he was able to calm their fear and restore their peace.

Some of you may be going through a rough time right now, feeling that you are sinking or drowning in your problems: a terrible diagnosis, an abusive relationship, a marriage gone bad, a drug-addicted child, an alcoholic spouse, dependent and sick elderly parents, the loss of a job or even bankruptcy. I am sure that some of you have had the feeling that God seems to be absent or asleep or disinterested in your situation.

Today's Gospel holds a message for you — the message that Jesus never sleeps and, when called on, can calm your terrified and worried heart and, in time, make your storms subside.

A 98-year-old friend of mine may have put it best when she said, "I'm not scared of dying. God has always taken care of me, and I trust that when the time comes, he will be there for me again."

August 3, 2006

The Sacredness of the Human Body

God formed man to be imperishable; the image of his own nature he made him. Wisdom 2

Most people are familiar with Michelangelo's Pieta, that nearly perfect sculpture from beautiful white marble picturing Mary holding the dead Jesus in her lap. People have admired its incredible beauty for nearly 500 years.

It was as close to flawless as any man-made piece of art could be — flawless that is, until May 21, 1972, when a 33-year-old Hungarian-born geologist, Laszlo Toth, attacked it with a sledge hammer, breaking Mary's arm at the elbow, knocking off a chunk of her nose and chipping one of her eyelids. It has been repaired and restored, but art historians — and art lovers — around the world cried that day.

As beautiful as it was, each human being is infinitely more beautiful in the eyes of God. "God formed man to be imperishable; the image of his own nature he made him." John records these words of Jesus: "We are God's children now; what we shall become has not yet come to light."

This is a great message, a needed message, because it seems that we are on a downhill slide when it comes to respect for ourselves and others. We often "take a sledgehammer" to the "image of God" within ourselves and others.

When respect for the "image of God" within every human being wanes, things such as abortion on demand and euthanasia become acceptable and even passed off as a contribution to society. When respect for the "image of God" within every human being is no longer acknowledged, self-destructive behavior and violence toward others starts being accepted as a normal part of life.

Recently on the Maury Povich Show, the topic of the day was people, most often women, who have been mutilated by their husbands or lovers through slashing or throwing acid into their faces. Reports of the physical, emotional and sexual abuse of others are rampant in our society.

Self-mutilation is also growing in popularity. Hardly a week goes by that there is not a show about young people who are into self-mutilation, cutting themselves with razors or knives.

Bulimia and anorexia among the young are so common that it is no longer news. On a less serious scale, excessive tattooing, body piercing and cosmetic surgery seem to tell us that people are growing more discontented with the beauty of the human body as it is.

It is not a surprise to me that one of the hottest topics among young seminarians is Pope John Paul II's "theology of the body." It is their response to the "culture of death" that they grew up on.

Part of our belief as Catholics is the sacredness of the human body. When we are baptized as babies, we are anointed with chrism as "children of God and royal heirs to his kingdom."

When we die, our bodies are incensed at our funerals as a sign of respect and reverence as former "temples of the Holy Spirit."

August 10, 2006

We are all Mentioned "In the Will"

We were chosen. We were adopted. We were sealed with the Holy Spirit, the first installment of our inheritance. Ephesians 1

Several years ago, I received a very ominous-looking personal letter from a law firm that I did not recognize.

I was scared to open it. My mind went wild.

Was I being sued for something? Had I been falsely accused of sexual abuse? Had I inadvertently forgotten to pay some debt? Had some legal glitch made the deed to my house invalid? I don't usually get mail from lawyers, so I expected the worse.

When I opened the envelope and nervously read the letter, I discovered to my surprise that an elderly woman from my days at the Cathedral of the Assumption had left $1,000 to me.

I did not recognize her name. I do not remember doing anything special for this woman; I don't even remember her funeral. It was not like inheriting money from one's parent. People usually expect such inheritances. This was a pure, undeserved, unexpected, unearned gift from a stranger who knew me and loved me.

When Jesus came to this earth announcing "good news," he himself was the "letter" sent to us by God with the news that we are "in the will." We are not "in the will" because we have done something special for God so as to deserve it, but simply because God loves us. This "letter" reads, "You, the good and the bad alike, are invited into my kingdom, not because you have done anything whatsoever to earn it, but simply because I love you." Jesus compared this gift that God offers us not to a check in mail, but to stumbling onto a buried treasure, something neither earned nor deserved.

Many of us today who identify ourselves as "Christian" have either not heard this "good news" or do not believe it, including many of those called to preach it to others. Some are downright skeptical and even go so far as to warn people not to believe it.

What if people really believed in the fundamental reality of God's unconditional love? We don't really know, because it hasn't been tried. Some "yes, but" this idea of God's radical and unconditional love to death, fearing that if people really believe it, they might go out and do whatever they please because "God will love them anyway."

This has not been my experience, neither personally nor as one called to preach. In studying the Gospels and from my own personal and pastoral experience, I believe that once people truly hear the "good news," it is so transforming that they choose to change their behaviors, toward themselves and others, as a grateful response to this undeserved and unearned love. They freely choose to conform their lives to the will of this loving God.

Such conviction does not make things easier, but down deep they know that they are "in the will" and that the "will" is irrevocable. It's not a matter of justice, but of love.

August 17, 2006

The Faith-Filled Act of Organ Donation

A person can have no greater love than to lay down one's life for one's friends. John 15:13

Do you have a Kleenex? May I borrow your pen? May I use your phone? Would you give me one of your kidneys?

Most of us would do what we could to help someone else, at least up to a point. How many of us would have the courage to undergo surgery to remove one of our kidneys so that someone else could continue to live?

Most of us are probably OK with this idea once we are dead, but while we are alive is something else. Yet there are some very generous and brave people among us who do this for others, most for family members, but some even for total strangers.

In August, I went to Jewish Hospital to visit two of my cousins on my father's side. My cousin, Jeannie Wathen, donated one of her kidneys to her sister, another cousin, Judy Vogt. One of the things I learned was that the process of giving of a kidney is a lot more painful than the process of receiving one. Yet, in spite of this, Jeannie told me that she "never had a second thought" when she knew she could be a donor.

There is a lot of cheap talk these days about love, but in my book, Jeannie is a real, modern-day hero, an example to all of us of what real love is all about. All major religions, including our own, approve of organ donation and consider it an act of charity.

Approximately 93,000 people in this country are candidates waiting for organ transplants. Thousands more are awaiting life-enhancing tissue transplants. Each day seventeen people in the United

States die while waiting for organ transplants. Every thirteen minutes, another person's name is added to the list. As of August 4, 2006, more than 12,000 transplants from more than 6,000 donors have been performed this year.

Most organ donation is done after death. We can either donate organs and tissues or donate our entire bodies to science. When it comes to organ and tissue donation, one of the easiest ways to do this is to sign the back of our driver's licenses. Another way is to discuss organ and tissue donation, in case of unexpected death, with our families.

One of the most interesting stories I have ever heard about donating organs, after death, for scientific research involves a community of nuns who have all donated their brains to scientific study because of their low occurrence of Alzheimer's disease. Once again, women religious are leading the way when it comes to new ways of giving themselves in service to others.

The Letter of James tells us quite bluntly what real love is all about. "Take the case, my brothers, of someone who has never done a single good act but claims to have faith. If good works do not go with faith, that faith is quite dead."

August 24, 2006

"Workaholism" can be a Serious Problem

Come away by yourselves to a deserted place. People were coming and going in great numbers, and they had no opportunity even to eat. Mark 6

It was the Fourth of July, a typical holiday for me. I was holed up in my house, sitting in front of my computer cranking out columns for The Record, yet another homily for Bellarmine, and an outline for a chapter for my tenth book. The doorbell rang, and one of my friends stepped across the threshold and said quite emphatically, "I've come to drag you out of your hole!"

I was actually enjoying what I was doing. Like Mozart, "When I am, as it were, completely myself, entirely alone, and of good cheer, it is on such occasions that my ideas flow best and most abundantly."

"I've come to drag you out of your hole!"

Even though I was enjoying myself, he was right. I find writing and public speaking to be "enjoyable" and regular, normal recreation and just killing time "hard work." I admit that I overdo it. I am notorious among my friends for my lack of a social life.

Even though I am entitled to one day a week off and four weeks of vacation a year, I often work on my day off and forget to plan a vacation until another year rolls around. Even when I do get away, I have outlined most of my books sitting on a beach chair, while on "vacation."

The story of Jesus' disciples coming home tired from preaching and teaching and healing is one near and dear to my heart. Jesus knew the "harvest was great and the laborers were few," but he also knew his disciples needed rest if they were going to last the long haul. This story has a lot to teach us on the upcoming Labor Day weekend.

St. Vincent de Paul said it this way: "Be careful to preserve your health. It is a trick of the devil, which he employs to deceive good souls, to invite them to do more than they are able, in order that they may no longer be able to do anything."

"Workaholics" live for their work, routinely spending many extra hours at work and often taking work home to complete. When work becomes the sole reason for a person's existence above more important things (such as family, friends and God), the issue becomes critical.

"Workaholism" can be a serious condition that can lead to the decline and destruction of families, to stress-related health problems and to a total loss of a spiritual life. When work becomes the sole reason for being — when it becomes the only thing we think about, the only thing that truly makes us happy — then it is time to "come away by yourself to a deserted place and rest awhile."

Healthy hard workers know the boundaries between work and personal time and can function normally when not at work, while workaholics have no personal time and cannot function well unless they are working.

August 31, 2006

Improving the Church,
One Person at a Time

*I urge you to live in a manner worthy of the call
you have received. Ephesians 4:1*

It is trendy these days to believe that if the leadership of church would only be more perfect, we as individual members would suddenly be more Christian. The truth of the matter is probably the other way around. If we individuals would be more Christian, the leadership of the church would no doubt improve as well.

If the church is weak, it is because it is made up of weak people. No church can be strong when too many of its members are weak.

There is something about us modern-day Catholics that makes us want to blame the weaknesses of the institution for our own lack of fidelity. "The scandal" has given innumerable Catholics a convenient excuse for ditching their own commitments to discipleship. "They failed, so now it's OK for me to give up," they say.

How convenient! Chesterton was right: "Christianity has not been tried and found wanting; it has been found difficult and not tried."

The thesis of my second book, *One Heart at a Time*, was that the church will be renewed when individual believers start living in a manner worthy of the call they have received, rather than waiting until there is some magic, institutional change that will suddenly turn us all into better Christians. The challenge in that book was for people to take their attention off the church as an institution and start placing it on themselves.

This is behind Paul's urging of the church members at Ephesus to live in a manner worthy of the call they received. The result of that kind of living, he believed, would bring the church unity and peace. He knew that the church would get better, one Christian at a time.

Sadly, the leadership of our church has been distracted in the last few years, trying to clean up a tragic scandal. There is a temptation to give in to feelings of anger and frustration. We must resist. This is a wake-up call for the whole church, leaders and members.

Every one of us has failed, in our own way, to live in a manner worthy of the call we have received. Our leadership is cleaning up its act, and we all need to clean up ours. This is a time to examine our own consciences and not just the consciences of others. It is our job to live in a manner worthy of the call we have received.

The question to all of us today is simple and direct. Do you consciously try to live a Christian life, or do you simply do what other people do? What are the principles that guide your life? Do you even know what manner of living is truly Christian? Are you committed to these principles, whether others fail to live them or not: your friends, your neighbors, even your church leaders? Will you live in a manner worthy of your calling?

September 7, 2006

We Live in a World of Choices

Decide today whom you will serve. Joshua 24

The word decision comes from the Latin meaning "to cut apart." When you "decide," when you "cut things apart" — something stays and something goes, something is chosen and something is rejected, something is embraced and something is pushed away.

We are asked to choose all day, every day. When we "decide," we "cut apart" one option from another so as to concentrate our energy in one area, rather than weakening it by spreading it too thin over too many areas. When we fail to "decide," we are often paralyzed and end up doing nothing.

The reading cited above is about decision and choice. Joshua asks the people to make a decision about committing themselves to the God of Israel. Arriving in a land sprinkled with other gods and with the temptation to stray from fidelity to the God of Israel, Joshua asks for a decision.

Joshua had asked the Israelites to remain faithful before, but here he is at the end of his life asking them yet again for fidelity. "Choose today whom you will serve. As for me and my household, we will serve the Lord."

This reading has an important message for us today, when people's word and commitments don't mean very much. We live in a world of the "latest best offer."

"I'll love you until someone better comes along, until you get fat and sick, until, until, until ..."

People used to do business with the shake of a hand. Now you have to call in the lawyers and witnesses because people will lie to your face. The Arabs have a saying, "Trust your camel, but tie it first." All this has made us a bit cynical and suspicious of each other.

When it comes to fidelity, doing what is right and doing what we have committed to do, a principled person decides what he will do according to a set of standards and values, while an opportunist decides what he will do according to whether it will bring him immediate satisfaction and gain, regardless of the long-term harm to himself or others.

The second thing about fidelity is that we have to practice it — we have to be faithful in small things before we can be faithful in big things. Fidelity is like weight lifting. You are able to lift heavy loads by lifting heavier and heavier loads over a long time.

The third thing about fidelity is that it is always fragile and, therefore, must be protected. It is not static, but fluid. Fidelity, like a baby, is fragile and needs constant care and feeding over many years.

We live in a world of choices. This is a blessing that carries great responsibility. We have a choice, yes, but also a responsibility to make good choices. Once we have made a choice, we have a responsibility to carry through on that choice, not just for our own good, but also for the good of the people around us.

September 14, 2006

"Rewinding" our Clocks for Service to God

Happy are you who find wisdom, you who gain understanding. When you lie down, you need not be afraid; when you rest, your sleep will be sweet. Proverbs 3:13,24

Predictions are a dime a dozen, and many of us assume that they will turn out to be true, especially if they come from an "authority."

One case in point was a Time magazine prediction back in the 1960s. Expert testimony was given to a subcommittee of the Senate on time management. The gist was that due to advances in technology, within 20 years or so, people would have to cut back radically on how many hours a week they worked or they would have to start retiring sooner.

The great challenge, they said, would be figuring out what to do with all the excess time.

Thirty years later, few of us would agree with that prediction. (Would that present predictions on the priest shortage turn out as badly!)

The reality of the situation is that we are always looking for ways to save time. We eat food at chain restaurants, not because it is great food, but because it is "fast" food. We can now eat in the car on our way to something else.

We even have "fast access DSL" so that we don't have to wait a minute or two for an Internet connection. Domino's Pizza was propelled to greatness when it promised to deliver in 30 minutes or less. "We don't sell pizza. We sell delivery," the company said. Catholics claw the walls or head for the parking lot if Mass goes longer than 50 minutes.

Many of us find ourselves in a continuous struggle to accomplish more things and participate in more events in less and less time. As much as we gripe and complain about it, most of us would not change if we could. It makes us feel important. We like the adrenaline rush. It means we don't have to feel lonely or unimportant.

But living life in a dead run is a sure sign of a disordered heart.

"Busy-ness" may have gotten worse since the time of Jesus, but it was a factor then, too. One passage I always laugh at is the one that says, "For many were coming and going, and they had no time even to eat." Jesus not only diagnosed the problem, he also prescribed a cure.

"Come away to a deserted place all by yourselves and rest a while."

St. Francis de Sales makes a good point in his Introduction to the Devout Life. "There is no clock, no matter how good it may be, that doesn't need resetting and rewinding twice a day, once in the morning and once in the evening. In addition, at least once a year it must be taken apart to remove the dirt clogging it, straighten out its bent parts, and repair those worn out. In like manner, every morning and evening a man who really takes care of his heart must rewind it for God's service."

September 21, 2006